JANUA LINGUARUM

STUDIA ·MEMORIAE
NICOLAI VAN WIJK DEDICATA

edenda curat

C. H. VAN SCHOONEVELD

Indiana University

Series Minor, 106

PROBLEMS OF TYPOLOGICAL AND GENETIC LINGUISTICS VIEWED IN A GENERATIVE FRAMEWORK

by

HENRIK BIRNBAUM

1970

MOUTON

THE HAGUE · PARIS

LIBRARY OF CONGRESS CATALOG CARD NUMBER: 70-123298

Printed in The Netherlands by Mouton & Co., Printers, The Hague.

PREFATORY NOTE

Of the three papers joined in this volume, the first and longest one has not previously appeared in print; the second one was first published in *Folia Linguistica* II, 1/2 (1969), 1-17, and is an extended version of a paper presented at the Tenth International Congress of Linguists, Bucharest, August 28-September 2, 1967; the third contribution appearing here for the first time in English is an extended and revised version of a paper originally published in Polish ("Rekonstrukcja wewnętrzna, kolejność synchronicznych reguł gramatyki syntetycznej i zagadnienie najdawniejszych stosunków między językami bałtyckimi a słowiańskimi") in the *International Journal of Slavic Linguistics and Poetics* XI (1968), 1-24. Included in the revised version of this paper is a short discussion of the paper by V.J. Zeps, "A Synchronic and Diachronic Order of Rules: Mutations of Velars in Old Church Slavonic" (*Approaches in Linguistic Methodology*, I. Rauch and C.T. Scott, eds., 145-151) and of the recent treatment of the Slavic palatalizations by N. Chomsky and M. Halle (*The Sound Pattern of English*, 420-430).

Written for different occasions, the three papers treating, in large measure, closely related matters necessarily display a certain amount of duplication in reasoning as well as exemplification. For this the author offers his apologies to the reader rather than attempting to cut the text of any of the original versions.

H. B.

CONTENTS

Prefatory Note   5

1. Deep Structure and Typological Linguistics   9

2. On Reconstruction and Prediction: Two Correlates of
   Diachrony in Genetic and Typological Linguistics . . . 71

3. Internal Reconstruction, Order of Synchronic Rules in
   Generative Grammar, and the Problem of Early Balto-
   Slavic Relations 92

Bibliography 123

DEEP STRUCTURE AND TYPOLOGICAL LINGUISTICS

En réalité, une typologie linguistique exhaustive est la tâche la plus grande et la plus importante qui s'offre à la linguistique. — En fin de compte, sa tâche est de répondre à la question: quelles structures linguistiques sont possibles, et pourquoi telles structures sont-elles possibles quand d'autres ne le sont pas? Ce faisant, elle doit, plus qu'aucune autre espèce de linguistique, s'approcher de ce qu'on pourrait appeler le problème de la nature du langage. Et, en dernier ressort, elle s'avérera hiérarchiquement supérieure à la linguistique génétique; seule en effet elle peut permettre de comprendre les lois générales selon lesquelles les langues changent et les possibilités de changement que comporte un type donné. C'est seulement par la typologie que la linguistique s'élève à des points de vue tout à fait généraux et devient une science.

Louis Hjelmslev, *Le langage*, 128-9

1. DEEP STRUCTURE AND THE SEMANTIC COMPONENT

One of the most significant trends in transformational theory so far has no doubt been characterized by the efforts to elaborate notions and devise rules by which the semantic component of linguistic structure could, in a reasonable and meaningful way, be incorporated into the general framework of generative grammar.[1] While the addition of a separate semantic component and

---

[1] Cf., for example, J.J. Katz and J.A. Fodor, "The Structure of a Semantic Theory", *Language* 39 (1963), 170-210 (reprinted in: *The Structure of Language: Readings in the Philosophy of Language*, J.A. Fodor, J.J. Katz [eds.], [Englewood Cliffs, N.J., 1964], 479-518); J.J. Katz and P.M. Postal, *An Integrated*

the attempts to relate it to the central, syntactic component at first seemed to raise some doubts and elicited not wholly unjustified criticism,[2] it soon became clear to generative grammarians that the boundary between syntax and semantics remains indeed largely fuzzy and ill-defined.[3] In particular, the emphasis placed on the distinction between a readily observable, sequentially arranged ('linear') surface structure and an underlying deep structure (with the latter representing the relationships obtaining between various semantic-categorial units in which the overt linguistic fabric is firmly anchored) has led to an intensified search for a finite set of universally ascertainable semantic elements or features and posited a number of special problems which, with some oversimplification, could perhaps be subsumed under the general question: how deep is deep structure? — suggesting, as it were, that the semantic-functional foundations of sentence structure (to say nothing of longer well-formed word strings and well-organized concatenations of clauses and sentences) may well reach far be-

---

Theory of Linguistic Descriptions (Cambridge, Mass., 1964); J.J. Katz, "Recent Issues in Semantic Theory", *Foundations of Language* 3 (1967), 124-194; N. Chomsky, "The Formal Nature of Language", Appendix A, in: E.H. Lenneberg, *Biological Foundations of Language* (New York, 1967), 397-442, esp. 404-405, 416-419; J.D. McCawley, "The Role of Semantics in a Grammar", in: *Universals in Linguistic Theory*, E. Bach, R.T. Harms (eds.), (New York, 1968), 124-169.

[2] Cf., in particular, U. Weinreich, "Explorations in Semantic Theory", in: *Current Trends in Linguistics*, T.A. Sebeok (ed.), Vol. III: *Theoretical Foundations* (The Hague, 1966), 395-477. See now also Y. Bar-Hillel, "Universal Semantics and Philosophy of Language: Quandaries and Prospects", in: *Substance and Structure of Language*, J. Puhvel (ed.), (Berkeley – Los Angeles, 1969), 1-21.

[3] Cf., for example, N. Chomsky, *Aspects of the Theory of Syntax* (Cambridge, Mass., 1965), 148-163; see further also *Idem, Topics in the Theory of Generative Grammar* (The Hague, 1966), 58-75; C.J. Fillmore, "The Case for Case", in: *Universals in Linguistic Theory*, 1-88, esp. 88 ("Closing Words"). For a semantic-categorial approach to the foundations of syntax from other premises, see also E. Koschmieder, "Die noetischen Grundlagen der Syntax", in: *Beiträge zur allgemeinen Syntax* (Heidelberg, 1965), 70-89 (first published as Heft 4 of the *Sitzungsberichte der Bayerischen Akademie der Wissenschaften, Phil.-hist. Klasse*, 1951). From a somewhat different standpoint and applied to actual (viz., Russian) linguistic data, see also Ju.D. Apresjan, *Èksperimental'noe issledovanie semantiki russkogo glagola* (Moscow, 1967), 23-35.

yond or, figuratively speaking, below the syntactic component. Put in slightly different terms, this search can be viewed as attempting to define the sizable, though limited inventory of irreducible semantic invariants presumably characteristic of all (natural) language.

In this context it ought to be pointed out that 'deep structure' is conceived here (and in the following) in its Chomskyan sense, a sense implicit, incidentally, also in Hockett's earlier usage of the terms 'surface' and 'deep grammar', with the difference, however, that Chomsky interprets the deep-to-surface structure correlation as an input-output device for sentence generation while Hockett simply ascertained, from an analytical point of view, existing deep-seated relationships not immediately discernible in any overt linguistic structure. This difference between Hockett's 'deep/surface grammar' and Chomsky's 'deep/surface structure' is comparable, therefore, in some measure to the difference existing between 'transformation' in Harris' sense (as a descriptive, 'taxonomic' device) and the same term in Chomsky's generative theory, this latter conceptual framework bearing considerable resemblance not only to Humboldt's vaguely formulated interpretation of language as 'creative' *energeia* (rather than merely *ergon*, i.e., the classifiable and segmentable linguistic data as such; a parallelism in conception, much acknowledged, if not overstated, by Chomsky) but also to the 'item-and-process' model (in contradistinction to the 'item-and-arrangement' model) of post-Bloomfieldian descriptive linguistics, as formulated by Hockett.[4] Chomsky's 'deep/surface

---

[4] Cf. C.F. Hockett, *A Course in Modern Linguistics* (New York, 1958), 246-252 ("Surface and Deep Grammar") and *passim*. Of Z. Harris' early work on transformations, cf. "Discourse Analysis", *Language* 28 (1952), 1-30, esp. 18-23; "Distributional Structure", *Word* 10 (1954), 146-162; and, in particular, "Co-occurrence and Transformation in Linguistic Structure", *Language* 33 (1957), 283-340 (all three papers are reprinted in: *The Structure of Language*, 355-383, esp. 372-378; 33-49; and 155-210). On Humboldt's characterization of language as *energeia* and its reemergence in generative grammar, see, for example, N. Chomsky, *Cartesian Linguistics* (New York 1966), 19 and 86-87; *Idem, Current Issues in Linguistic Theory* (The Hague, 1964), 17-21. On the 'item-and-process' model of linguistic description, see C.F. Hockett, "Two Models of Grammatical Description", *Word* 10 (1954), 210-234; for some com-

structure' dichotomy is, moreover, closely related to Humboldt's well-known distinction between *innere* and *äussere Form* (with reference to the sentence as a linguistic unit) and, indirectly, also to Wittgenstein's *Tiefen-* vs. *Oberflächengrammatik* (as used in symbolic logic).[5] 'Deep structure' and 'surface structure', respectively, are in other words not to be confused here with a different, though also current, more vague and metaphoric usage of these terms, roughly corresponding to the distinction of varying 'levels of abstraction' (this concept in itself being indeed a very useful one in linguistic analysis), thus allowing for increasingly 'deeper' structures (or levels of representation) in a sense analogous to increasingly 'higher' 'levels of abstraction'. This metaphoric usage of the term 'deep' and 'surface structure' lacks, for one thing, the clear-cut relation to the content vs. expression dichotomy inherent in the Chomskyan sense of these terms.[6] Moreover, it permits one

---

ments on the reception of Hockett's paper, cf. *Idem, The State of the Art* (The Hague, 1968), 29-30. Cf. further also the recent critical statement by R.A. Hall, Jr. (in: *An Essay on Language* [Philadelphia, 1968], 79): "Transformational-generative grammar is simply an extension of the item-and-process approach to all items of linguistic structure, whether it is appropriate to them or not, and with an insistence on setting up intermediate steps in which only one item is changed at a time, whether the intermediate steps thus assumed exist or not."

[5]   Cf. N. Chomsky, *Aspects of the Theory of Syntax*, 198-199; L.Wittgenstein, *Philosophical Investigations* (Oxford, 1953), 168. For some sharp criticism of the whole deep/surface structure concept and its foundation in universal grammar (or the theory of linguistic universals), see R.A. Hall, Jr., *An Essay on Language*, 5-9 (against idealism and rationalism, particularly of the French 17th-18th cc. kind, in linguistics), 52-55, 71-72, 75, 77, and 116, and 129, 149 (condemning the 'pseudo-logic' universal Port Royal grammar).

[6]   For the notion of 'level of abstraction' in linguistic analysis, see, for example, B. Malmberg, *Structural Linguistics and Human Communication* (New York–Berlin, 1963), 80-81, 96-117, esp. 111-112, 125 (mostly as applied to different phonological levels of abstraction). A fundamental distinction of two levels of abstraction underlies also, to take a relevant example, S. K. Šaumjan's so-called two-level principle (or system of concepts) in its application to phonological as well as general linguistic analysis (*dvuxstupenčataja teorija fonologii* and *dvux-stupenčataja teorija poroždajuščix grammatik*). As is well known, Šaumjan distinguishes between a 'genotype' (or 'construct') and a 'phenotype' (or 'observation') level of abstraction. Cf. in particular his paper "Concerning the Logical Basis of Linguistic Theory", in: *Proceedings of the Ninth International Congress of Linguists*, H.G. Lunt (ed.), (The Hague, 1964), 155-160, and his book *Strukturnaja lingvistika* (Moscow, 1965). A recent example of the meta-

to assume a number of superimposed underlying structural levels (of increasingly greater 'depth'), an assumption fundamentally alien to the deep structure concept of the Chomskyan brand. This difference is of particular significance for our subsequent reasoning since in the following discussion an essential modification of the notion of deep structure in the Chomskyan sense will be proposed, claiming the usefulness, if not necessity, of adding a new dimension to deep structure by distinguishing in it several interrelated but largely autonomous layers or strata. This differentiated, stratificational view of (Chomskyan) deep structure ought therefore not to be taken for the multilayered metaphoric notion of deep structure just referred to.

As a result of the general trend toward a generative semantic framework, a new, slightly modified model of generative grammar seems now to be taking shape. This model can be thought of as comprising three interdependent components:

(1) A SEMANTIC COMPONENT which will define the relations obtaining between semantic (including categorial) units or, rather,

---

phoric (non-Chomskyan) usage of the terms 'surface' and 'deep structure', roughly equaling the gamut of varying levels of abstraction, can be found in D. S. Worth's insightful Prague Congress paper "'Surface Structure' and 'Deep Structure' in Slavic Morphology", in: *American Contributions to the Sixth International Congress of Slavists*, Vol. I: *Linguistic Contributions*, H. Kučera (ed.), (The Hague–Paris, 1968), 395-427. Similarly, Worth now also uses the terms 'phonological deep structure' and 'deep phonology' in a sense where, strictly speaking, a definition such as 'a more abstract level of phonological representation' (or 'symbolization') would seem more appropriate; cf. his most recent article "On the Morphophonemics of the Slavic Verb", *Slavia* XXXIX (1970), 1-9. Notice, incidentally, that the range of increasingly higher levels of abstraction in linguistic analysis includes, among other transitions, also the step from a highly abstract level of symbolization (viz., the morphophonemic level, in traditional terminology, or its equivalent) to the relatively least abstract level of semantic unit representation (viz., the morphemic level, in traditional terminology, or its equivalent). However, in passing from one level of abstraction to another, this particular transition is in itself in no way more significant than, say, the step from the subphonemic to the phonemic level (assuming here, for the sake of the argument, that the existence of the latter need not be challenged) or from the phonemic to the morphophonemic level. In the deep/surface structure distinction (in the Chomskyan sense), the content/expression (or semantic/symbolization) dichotomy, while also implying a change of level of abstraction, is, on the other hand, the only relevant one.

hierarchically ordered clusters of semantic features (such as, e.g., [THING], [CONCRETE], [COUNTABLE], [ANIMATE], [HU-MAN], [PERSONAL], [MALE], [ADULT]; [PREDICATION], [AGENT], [DEFINITE], [ACTION], [PATIENT-ORIENTED], [TIME-DETERMINED], [ASPECT-DETERMINED], etc.[7] In

[7] The semantic (and categorial) feature specifications given here as examples must be considered tentative; they are partly overlapping, whereas in a definite list they could, of course, not overlap. A rigorously defined set of such universal features could contain only mutually exclusive ones (wherever hierarchically equivalent) and all-inclusive ones (wherever at hierarchically different level). However, the hierarchical ordering of features is not necessarily a priori fixed but may indeed vary. For example, [MALE] can have priority over [ADULT] or even [HUMAN] where a subgrouping of male people (and animals) according to age or maturity is considered and has to be verbalized, while [ADULT] would take precedence over [MALE] in the case of subspecifying by sex and/or gender previously unspecified adults, and so forth. Clearly, certain feature specifications, such as [ANIMATE], would normally have hierarchical priority over, say [HUMAN], and thus include or subsume certain (sub)specifications like [HUMAN] or [ADULT]. While [HUMAN] and [PERSONAL] may be considered as overlapping or even partly synonymous in one sense, [PERSON-AL] can also be conceived as a categorial subspecification under [PREDICA-TION], the latter being the fundamental sentence-marker (with its opposite, [−PREDICATION] = [NON-PREDICATION] or [NOMINATION] serving as the basic marker of such well-formed word strings which do not form sentences). To devise a set of opposite ('non-') features may be superfluous if the specified features are marked for presence (+) or absence (−), respectively. Notice further that some of the tentative feature specifications quoted are suggestive of, but not identical with, certain grammatical categories (word classes, clause members, functions), e.g., [AGENT] of 'subject', [PATIENT] of 'object' (and both of 'noun' or 'pronoun'), [ACTION] of 'verb', [PATIENT-ORIENTED] of 'transitive' or 'passive', [TIME-DETERMINED] of '(marked for) tense', etc. For some more thoughts on componential analysis and universal semantics, see, for example, J. Lyons, *Introduction to Theoretical Linguistics* (Cambridge, 1968), 470-481. Progress of related work has been reported in recent Soviet and Polish linguistic studies (by I.A. Mel'čuk, A.K. Žolkovskij, Ju.D. Apresjan, and other Soviet linguists; by A. Bogusławski, I. Bellert, A. Wierzbicka; for bibliographical references to Soviet work in this field, see the literature cited by Ju.D. Apresjan, *op.cit.*, 241-244; for some references to contributions by Polish linguists, see the titles quoted in *Studies in Slavic Linguistics and Poetics in Honor of Boris O. Unbegaun*, R. Magidoff, G.Y. Shevelov, J.S.G. Simmons, K. Taranovski, J.E. Allen III (eds.), (New York, 1968), 28 (in note 6 of my contribution "On Deep Structure and Loan Syntax in Slavic"). For a glossematic approach to structural semantics, see in particular L. Hjelmslev, "Pour une sémantique structurale", in: *Essais linguistiques* (Copenhagen, 1959) (= *TCLC* XII), 96-112 (title of original paper: "Dans quelle mesure les

addition to defining the relations between semantic entities (or complexes of semantic features), the semantic component will include a lexicon of the given language, i.e., an inventory of its lexical items; for some more details, see below (with note 10).

(2) A TRANSFORMATIONAL COMPONENT which will convert the semantic deep structure representations into surface structure representations.

(3) A PHONOLOGICAL (or SYMBOLIZATION) COMPONENT which will contain a partially ordered set of rules by which 'systematic phonemic' (i.e., roughly morphophonemic, in the traditional sense of the term) representations are converted into a 'systematic phonetic' (i.e., subphonemic or modified distinctive feature) symbolization, taking into account the cyclical character of such rules as well as the labeled bracketings of the surface structure. (Notice, by the way, that rewriting a largely morphophonemic notation to a phonetic or feature notation, as performed by the rules of the phonological component, implies a switching from a 'higher' to a 'lower' 'level of abstraction' as regards the representation of the actual phonation — a switching which has nothing to do, however, with converting deep structure into surface structure as transformational generative theory conceives of these terms.)

Granted the fact that Chomskyan linguistics from its very inception has stressed the generative ('creative') character of grammar, i.e., grammar in the broadest sense conceived as a device or mechanism for the prediction and/or formal characterization of an infinite number of well-formed ('grammatical') sentences of a given language, and therefore has placed particular emphasis on the notion of 'rule of grammar' which, among other things, accounts for the need to isolate a separate transformational component (a principle to some degree anticipated not only by the 'item-and-process' model referred to previously but also by Sapir's mentalistic approach to language), the outlined modified framework of genera-

---

significations des mots peuvent-elles être considérées comme formant une structure?", in: *Proceedings of the Eighth International Congress of Linguists* [Oslo, 1958], 636-654).

tive grammar undoubtedly bears some resemblance to the dichotomy of content (corresponding roughly to the semantic component)
vs. expression (largely equaling the phonological or symbolization
component), as this dichotomy was conceived by one of the greatest
theoreticians of structural, 'taxonomic' (nongenerative) linguistics,
Louis Hjelmslev. In this context it should be noted, however, that
this particular content vs. expression dichotomy, articulated by
Hjelmslev, represents but a modification and reinterpretation of
the Saussurian distinction of *le signifié* and *le signifiant*, in turn
going back to earlier similar contrastings in Western philosophical
thought; cf. the medieval opposition *significatum* vs. *significans* or
the contrasting of *sēmainomenon* with *sēmainon*, *noēton* with
aisthēton in Stoic doctrine. In Hjelmslev's theory the two planes,
content and expression, are in principle not related by any one-
to-one correspondences but must rather be viewed as autonomous
and independent of each other. Nonetheless, a structural and typological parallelism obtains between the two planes; it manifests
itself in the so-called commutation test, amounting, in short, to
the contention that any linguistically relevant (distinctive) correlation in the content plane implies or has relation ('both-and function') to a concomitant correlation in the expression plane, and
vice versa.[8] Put in somewhat different terms, this insight was
reached and put to practice already by members of the Prague
School of the late 20's and the 30's whose great traditions are
carried on by the present group of linguists of an older as well as
younger generation centered in Prague. Roman Jakobson, instrumental in building and bridging the Prague and MIT Schools
of Linguistics, has, by contrasting sound and meaning as the two
fundamental components of linguistic structure, pointed to a
dichotomy which (while articulated and interpreted by earlier
schools of philosophical and linguistic thought) now, again, seems

---

[8]   Cf. L. Hjelmslev, *Prolegomena to a Theory of Language* [Rev. English ed.],
(Madison, 1961), *passim*, esp. 47-60; on 'commutation' esp. 73-74; *Idem*, "La
stratification du langage", in: *Essais linguistiques*, 36-68 (originally appeared
in *Word* 10 [1954], 163-188).

to stand out as that of the two basic conceptual frameworks of any valid theory of language.[9]

While it is true, then, that the semantic component, including a good portion of what was previously assigned to the syntactic component, and the phonological component reemerge as the two most significant parts of linguistic structure, and the once central syntactic component is now being reduced to essentially the transformational (sub)component providing a mechanism for the conversion of semantically interpreted deep structure units (categories) and non-linear configurations into elements (segments), ultimately yielding sequentially strung sounds (including some suprasegmental prosodic features), it is equally important to point out that the semantic and phonological components, respectively, ought not to be confused with deep and surface structure as such.[10] This latter

---

[9]   See, when available, R. Jakobson's much-awaited book *Sound and Meaning*, summing up his thought on the foundations of linguistic structure; cf. further his paper "Quest for the Essence of Language", *Diogenes* 51 (Fall 1965), 21-37. For some modification of the sound-meaning model of language, see N. Chomsky, "The Formal Nature of Language", *Biological Foundations*, esp. 397-399.

[10]   In effect, this reevaluation and splitting up of the syntactic component implies that the base component, consisting of two parts, the categorial system and the lexicon, is transferred or reassigned to the semantic component. Thus the semantic component would now not only carry out, as in Chomsky's theory (in its presently known stage), the mapping of deep structures onto semantic representations but also generate the deep structures determined by the categorial system and the lexicon (i.e., by the base component, in Chomsky's theory heretofore considered part of the syntactic component). The conversion of deep structures into surface structures is performed by the transformational component (which now would achieve independent status), and the symbolization of surface structures by means of phonetic representations is implemented by the phonological component. For an account of Chomsky's recent thinking on the structure of the syntactic component (as he to date is known to conceive it), see his discussion in "The Formal Nature of Language", *Biological Foundations*, 419-434. It should perhaps be pointed out that the suggested new subdivision of a generative model of language, eliminating a syntactic component as such but retaining an independent transformational component, is primarily motivated by the realization of the artificiality of drawing a sharp, though largely arbitrary, line between lexical-categorial ('semantic') and functional (grammatical, 'syntactic') entities and relations, with deep structure belonging to the syntactic component. For recent developments of the deep structure concept, including some questioning of its very validity, cf. further, for example, C.J. Fillmore, "The Case for Case"; J.D. McCawley, "The Role of Semantics" (esp.

distinction is of a fundamentally different order than that between sound and meaning, expression and content.

---

165 ff.); *Idem*, "Concerning the Base Component of a Transformational Grammar", *Foundations of Language* 4 (1968), 243-269; G. P. Lakoff and J. R. Ross, "Is Deep Structure Necessary?" (Cambridge, Mass., 1967) [duplicated]; G. Lakoff, "Instrumental Adverbs and the Concept of Deep Structure", *Foundations of Language* 4 (1968), 4-29. See, in addition, also W. L. Chafe, "Language as Symbolization", *Language* 43 (1967), 57-91, taking somewhat different premises as his point of departure and adopting a dichotomous content/expression model with a further (likewise Hjelmslevian) substance/form subdivision where content substance = experience, expression substance = sound, and content form implies deep-to-surface semology and expression form initial-to-final symbolization (see esp. 74, fig. 3). Notice, further, that Chafe's view also obliterates the distinction between the syntactic and the semantic components of transformational-generative theory and that "higher degrees of abstractness can only be attributed to surface semology and initial symbolization, and to the symbolization link between them which lies at the apex of remoteness from both experiential and acoustic data" (*op. cit.*, 88). By contrast, "transformational linguists have always characterized deep structure as 'highly abstract'" (*ibid.*).

Finally, in this context it should be stressed that the minimal entities or 'features' of the semantic component, also referred to as 'semantic markers', said to represent 'conceptual elements', ought not to be conceived in an oversimplified, 'atomistic' fashion (as was the case in Katz-Fodor's early version of a new theory of semantics); for some criticism, see Y. Bar-Hillel, "Universal Semantics", esp. 2-6. In particular, Bar-Hillel, speaking from the logician's vantage point, claims that what all recent attempts in semantic theory "missed (with the partial exception of Weinreich) was that meaning relations between linguistic entities are essentially deducibility relations and, therefore, logical relations" (*ibid.*, 2). Moreover, he suggests (*ibid.*, 6) that "nowhere does Katz show any awareness of the importance of semantic fields, a conception that makes it abundantly clear that, for innumerable terms, no individual, but only a collective, meaning specification is possible. His neglect is the more amazing since Chomsky has shown full awareness of this importance, though he apparently has had no time to discuss the topic at greater length"; whereupon follows a quote from Chomsky's *Aspects*, 164: "We have just seen that this account is oversimplified in the case of semantic features, further structure being necessary in the lexicon to account for field properties." — For further discussion of complexities in the structure of the semantic component (or the base subcomponent of the syntactic component in standard generative theory), see U. Weinreich, "Problems in the Analysis of Idioms", in: *Substance and Structure of Language*, 23-81, esp. 46-61, with diagram (25) ("Idioms in a Generative Framework") and 71-78, with diagram (33) ("Some Further Implications"). On 'idiomaticization' and 'metaphoricization', see also W. L. Chafe, "Language as Symbolization", 74-79.

2. THE STRATIFICATION OF DEEP STRUCTURE

My own view of linguistic structure as a functioning system bears, in more than one respect, a fairly close resemblance to Chafe's recent modification of Hjelmslev's multidichotomous concept of language briefly referred to. Clearly, 'form' in the Hjelmslevian sense is the equivalent of what by many students of language is understood as '(linguistic) structure', according to Hjelmslev, the only legitimate object of linguistics or, rather, of any theory of language viewed as a structure *sui generis*.

By removing from the Chomskyan syntactic component both the base subcomponent (consisting, in turn, of the categorial system and the lexicon) and deep structure, generated by the base, and reassigning these subcomponents and the operations they carry out to the accordingly expanded semantic component (thus reducing the syntactic component in effect to the transformational component), the mapping ('interpretation') of deep structure onto semantic representation (or, put in slightly different terms, the correlating of deep structures with their semantic representations) in Chomsky's model of the structure of a generative grammar would have to be incorporated into the deep-to-surface semology rearrangements performed in Chafe's model by his 'semological mutation rules', with the important difference, however, that the direction of the process in Chafe's model is reversed as compared to Chomsky's deep structure-to-semantic component operation.[11] On the other hand, compare now also Chomsky's recent insistence that no 'direction of mapping' or 'order of steps of generation' can or, indeed, should be established; for discussion, see Postscript. Primarily, though, Chafe's 'semological mutation rules' would correspond to the — to be sure, complex — operations performed by Chomsky's transformational component, yielding 'surface structure' or, to be exact, a level of surface syntactic representation whose existence (or, rather, necessary positing) is generally acknowledged also by those (younger generation) transformationalists

[11] Cf. N. Chomsky, "The Formal Nature of Language", esp. 420, with diagram (13); W. L. Chafe, "Language as Symbolization", 73-79, esp. 74, with figure 3.

who have begun to question the legitimacy of the deep structure concept as such.[12] The 'initial symbolization' structure in Chafe's model, representing, one might say, the 'input' of the 'expression' (or 'symbolization') 'form' as a whole (i.e., 'surface semology' after the application of a set of 'symbolization rules'), is thus in many ways the equivalent of Chomsky's 'surface structure' or, in more precise terms, the level of surface syntactic representation (i.e., sequentially arranged 'formatives') on which the P rules of the phonological component operate (corresponding to Chafe's 'phonological mutation rules'[13]). Yet there is a significant difference in the two views, which therefore creates some difficulty for any attempt to closely correlate the two conceptual frameworks or to translate, as it were, a concept of one theory into that of the other.

The preceding brief juxtaposition of Chomsky's and Chafe's views of linguistic structure was therefore merely intended to indicate some of the points where my own concept of language as a functioning system more closely coincides with Chafe's than with that held by Chomsky (but obviously no longer by some of the younger generation transformationalists), at least until quite recently. See Postscript, pp. 62-70, below.

However, given that deep structure as a whole (obliterating the distinction between semantic vs. syntactic deep structure) be considered part of the (expanded) semantic component, there is one aspect of this structure where I believe myself to be in closer agreement with the transformationalist view than with that of Chafe. This aspect is related to the universal semantic elements and their relationships, constituting the very deep structure of a particular language. Since, in my view, it is not possible to make a clear-cut distinction between, on the one hand, minimal (invariant) SEMANTIC units proper, yielding, in some hierarchical combination, lexical items of the type *boy* (representing a clustering of such semantic features as [+ANIMATE], [+HUMAN], [+MALE], [−ADULT], as well as others) and, on the other

---

[12]   Cf., for example, J.D. McCawley, "The Role of Semantics in a Grammar", esp. 165.
[13]   Cf. W.L. Chafe, "Language as Symbolization", 67-73.

hand, minimal CATEGORIAL units, yielding, in some combination, syntactic units (often, though by no means always, to be embodied in lexical units) such as 'indirect object' (involving a combination of some categorial features such as [+ PREDICATION], [+ PA-TIENT-ORIENTED], [+ PATIENT] or [− AGENT], [− DI-RECT], etc.) — which, incidentally, is one of the reasons why, as I see it, deep structure as a whole ought indeed to be considered part of the semantic component — the deep/surface semology distinction, as introduced by Chafe, does not, in my view, reflect a valid subdivision of the semantic component. Even if we are to admit that the set of minimal semantic features (in the broad sense; roughly corresponding to Hjelmslev's *figurae* of the content plane),[14] while universal and finite, nonetheless will amount to a considerable number (so that any comparison or parallelism suggested with a rigorously restricted set of universal phonological 'distinctive features' in the Jakobsonian sense loses most of its significance), semantic deep structure will remain highly abstract. The term 'deep structure', then, will be retained as indicating greater 'depth' in relation to the sequentially arranged surface structure, but not in relation to the componential elements ('semantic features') of which deep structure is made up. In other words, deep structure (the usefulness of which concept, if qualified, I continue to recognize) is here to be understood as the particular combination of minimal semantic elements ('lexical' as well as 'nonlexical' or 'categorial' in a more traditional sense) which underlie surface structure and its phonetic interpretation, to be sure, without any specific syntagmatic-linear order matching the latter's sequential arrangements and constraints.

While I thus would favor, with some qualifications, the retention of Chomskyan deep structure, it is another fundamental aspect of this concept of transformational theory that I find in urgent need of revision. I am referring here to the claim of deep structure essentially representing a set of language universals (or invariables).

---

[14]   Cf. L. Hjelmslev, *Prolegomena to a Theory of Language*, 46 (where, however, the Danish linguist speaks — erroneously, in my opinion — of but "a handful of *figurae*"); cf. further in particular *ibid.*, 70-73.

There can, of course, be little doubt that the minimal semantic elements (features) of which the units entering deep structure are made up have universal validity, even if every (natural) language does not avail itself of every ascertainable or conceivable semantic feature. Also, different languages may utilize a semantic feature in different ways. Thus, it seems safe to assume, for example, that the feature [+ PREDICATION] will be inherent in each sequence definable as 'sentence'. [+ PREDICATION], in turn, can be thought of as further specifiable in terms of [+ ACTION] or [− ACTION] (the latter equaling, say, [+ STATE]) or some comparable semantic dichotomy. [+ ACTION] can perhaps be generalized in English by the fairly abstract verb *do* while [− ACTION] (or [+ STATE]) would correspond to either *be* or *have* (cf., to illustrate this reducible duality, English 'I have a pencil' = Russian *U menja karandaš*, literally 'With/At me (is) a pencil'; 'I had a pencil' = *U menja byl karandaš*, literally 'With/At me was a pencil'). The difference between two word strings such as *the small house* and *the house is small* can therefore, as is generally recognized, be characterized as that between [− PREDICATION] (or [+ NOMINATION]) and [+ PREDICATION], respectively, only the latter one forming a sentence. In turn, the [+ PREDICATION] feature of this particular sentence would then need to be further specified as [− ACTION] (or [+ STATE]), and so forth. Likewise, it can be assumed that features such as [MALE] and [FEMALE], whether formalized in a particular linguistic structure as grammatical gender ('masculine' vs. 'feminine') or not, as well as [± ANIMATE], [± HUMAN], etc., are inherent in all human speech, although they frequently may be suspended (which amounts to remaining unspecified); cf. words such as *parent* or *child*, or, more particularly, German *Geschwister*, Swedish *syskon* 'brother(s) and/or sister(s)'. Again, for example, [MALE], [FEMALE] are but features subspecifying the superordinate feature [+ SEX-DETERMINED] (or simply 'marked for [SEX]'). In this context it should be noted that there are languages, like Hungarian, for example, which do not specify the feature [SEX-DETERMINED] at all, so that sex membership (in cases of natural sex) can only be deduced contextually. Similarly, [DEFINITE] is at best indirectly (contextually) expressed in languages such as Latin or Russian, lacking a definite article. Cf., for example, Russian *Ja ne vižu devuški* 'I don't see a/the girl' vs. *Ja ne vižu devušku* 'I don't see *the* girl'; or 'definiteness' implicit in the combination with a governing quantitative-partitive word, e.g., *mnogie iz devušek* 'many of *the* girls'. (I am indebted to my colleague M. Flier for drawing my attention to the above Russian examples.) All this, and many similar instances of nonspecification or partial suspension of otherwise existing specification in a language, does not, however, change the fundamental fact that the minimal semantic elements or features thus hierarchically combining into notions and concepts inherent in lexical items (as well as certain all-sentence-characteristic categories) are universal. The same claim seems applicable not only to the semantic features as such but also to many of the clusters of semantic features making up some basic, universal notions (such as, say, *father*, represented by features such as [MALE], [ADULT], [PROGENITOR], and perhaps some others) while in other instances, the classification of even the most fundamental concepts of reality may vary or overlap from language to language (cf., for example, 'hand' vs. 'arm' = Russian *ruka*; 'foot' vs. 'leg' = Russian *noga*, the Russian concepts obviously being less specified by at least one semantic feature definable, perhaps, as [EXTREME]).[15]

However, while justified when it comes to the ultimate, irreducible semantic features and at least partly justified also when it comes to the very concepts into which some of these features combine (or cluster in a particular hierarchical order), this universality claim is, in my view, only to a very limited extent valid when it comes to deep structure proper, i.e., to the very relationships into which these semantic features and units enter within a larger semantic-categorial entity as manifested, at the surface, in the makeup and the phonetic shape of a sentence. It is, in other words, in this point that I cannot share Chomsky's and some of his

---

[15] For some additional examples of semantic 'overlap' between languages, see also L. Hjelmslev, *Prolegomena to a Theory of Language*, 52-54; *Idem, Essais linguistiques*, 103-105.

followers' claim that deep structure is largely universal.[16] To be
sure, as was already stated, some structural characteristics underlying all sentences and in particular [PREDICATION], entering
into specific relationships with such other features as [AGENT]
(expressed normally by a 'subject'), [PATIENT] (suggesting an
'object'), [PERSONAL] (embodied frequently, along with [PREDI-
CATION], in a 'finite verb form'), to the extent these features are
present in one of the semantic units of the sentence, must no doubt

---

[16] Cf., for example, N. Chomsky, *Aspects of the Theory of Syntax*, 117-118;
see further also, for example, R. Růžička, *Studien zur Theorie der russischen
Syntax* (Berlin, 1966), 19-20. In all fairness it should be noted, however, that
R.A. Hall, Jr., when criticizing transformational generative theory, somewhat
exaggerates the universality claim for deep structure (traceable back to universal
grammar of the Port Royal type) as attributed to Chomsky and his followers;
cf. R.A. Hall, Jr., *An Essay on Language*, 52 ("that there is a 'deep' structure
underlying this 'surface' structure, which is aprioristically declared to be the
same for all human language"), 71 ("However, we get around this difficulty by
assuming [*a priori*, without demonstration] that the 'deep structure' of all languages is identical."), and elsewhere. A closer reading of the relevant passages
in Chomsky and others will show that their formulations actually are a good
deal more cautious. Cf., for example, N. Chomsky, *Aspects...*, 117: "To say
that formal properties of the base will provide the framework for the characterization of universal categories is to assume that MUCH OF THE STRUCTURE
OF THE BASE IS COMMON TO ALL LANGUAGES. — ... INSOFAR AS ASPECTS OF THE
BASE STRUCTURE ARE NOT SPECIFIC TO A PARTICULAR LANGUAGE, they need not
be stated in the grammar of this language" (emphasis added). See also N.
Chomsky, "The Formal Nature of Language", 436-437: "Traditional universal
grammar tried to demonstrate, on the basis of what information was then
available, that deep structures vary little from language to language. — ...
Actually, modern 'anthropological linguistics' has provided little evidence that
bears on the assumption of uniformity of deep structures, and insofar as the
universality of categories is concerned, conclusions rather like the traditional
ones are commonly accepted in practice in descriptive work." Cf. further also
R. Růžička, *Theorie der russischen Syntax*, 20: "Die Basis weist offenbar viele
formale Eigenschaften auf, die universelle Geltung beanspruchen können." —
Thus it would perhaps be more fair to say that much emphasis has been placed
by the generative grammarians on the 'traditional' assumption of deep structure being allegedly predominantly universal, i.e., common to all languages
without, however, altogether denying some (if only insignificant and, to be sure,
unspecified) leeway for language-individual variations of deep structure. It is,
therefore, against this deemphasizing of deep structure as characteristic only
of a certain group ('type') of languages or of only one particular language that
my subsequent remarks are directed.

be considered language-universal.[17] But this does not necessarily hold true of a great number of other characteristics of deep structure underlying the surface structure of a sentence in a particular language. Many such deep structure characteristics can be shown to belong not to all (natural) language but only to a specific language type (however defined; see below) while still others may turn out to be ascertainable only in the covert deep structure of one particular language.

It is out of such considerations that I have suggested elsewhere that deep structure, too, be conceived of as forming a multilayered system of levels of various SEMANTIC 'depth', thus interpreting the notion 'deep' not merely as synonymous with 'underlying' (with respect to surface structure) but as ranging over its own dimension of greater or lesser generality as well.[18] More specifically, I proposed to distinguish between at least three basic degrees of 'depth' in Chomskyan deep structure, namely:

(1) Deep structure of least 'depth'; for this layer the term 'shallow' or even better perhaps, utilizing an already existing

---

[17] Still this should not be understood as suggesting that the [PREDICATION] feature of all sentences in all languages is UNIFORMLY integrated into various complex deep structures. It may suffice to point to the difference between one- and two-membered sentences, respectively (i.e., subjectless, 'impersonal' sentences as opposed to sentences of the 'subject' + 'predicate' type, with the subject either explicit in the surface structure as a noun or pronoun, or implicit in the verb, usually by means of its grammatical form; cf. *I love, you love, [he, she, it] loves* as compared to Latin *amo, amas, amat*), and also to the fact that, within [PREDICATION], the [ACTION]–[PATIENT] relationship may be expressed, in the surface, by different morphological means, not necessarily requiring the use of separate word forms (cf., for example, Hungarian *szeretek* 'I love', *szeretlek* 'I love you [sing. or plur.; informal address]', *szeretem* 'I love him, her, it; them; you [formal address]').

[18] Cf. G. Birnbaum (H. Birnbaum), "Obščeslavjanskoe nasledie i inojazyčnye obrazcy v strukturnyx raznovidnostjax staroslavjanskogo predloženija", *American Contributions to the Sixth International Congress of Slavists*, Vol. I: *Linguistic Contributions*, H. Kučera (ed.), (The Hague–Paris, 1968), 29-63, esp. 51-52. Notice, incidentally, that Postal has used the terms 'superficial' and 'underlying structure', respectively, in the same sense as 'surface' and 'deep structure'; cf. P. M. Postal, "Underlying and Superficial Linguistic Structure", *Harvard Educational Review* 34 (1964), 246-266; now reprinted (with slight revisions) in: *Language and Learning*, J. A. Emig, J. T. Fleming, H. M. Popp (eds.), (New York, 1966), 153-175.

notion, INFRASTRUCTURE (alluding to the immediately UNDERlying nature of this structure) could be introduced. 'Infrastructure' is least generalized and always language-specific (see below).

(2) An intermediate layer or rather a set of various intervening strata of deep structure characterized by some greater generality and 'depth' than the most 'shallow', language-specific 'infrastructure'. These differently defined deep strata of linguistic structure will be determined by certain deep-seated properties characteristic of a variety of particular, typologically definable groups of languages. As an overall cover term for these deep strata we can therefore use the label TYPOLOGICAL DEEP STRUCTURE. Since the number of typologically defined groupings to which a particular language can belong may vary considerably, the number of ascertainable typological deep structure levels in that language will vary accordingly. To take an example, Bulgarian is an Indo-European language, but also a Slavic language, as well as being more specifically a South Slavic language. In addition, it is a Balkan language, in the narrow linguistic, "Sprachbund" sense of the term,[19] an analytic language rather than a language of the synthetic type, and so forth. Thus it constitutes a member language of a great variety of language types, each characterized by its particular set of deep structure properties. The historical reasons for a language's membership in a group of typologically linkable languages are of merely incidental interest and ultimately irrelevant for any synchronic typological language classification. Such historical reasons can lie in genetic relationship (Indo-European, Slavic, South Slavic, in the instance adduced) or areal adjacency (in this case, Balkan) leading to a considerable extent of convergence, further enhanced, perhaps, by common linguistic sub-, ad-, or superstrata as a leveling and integrating force; furthermore, in a far-reaching degree of underlying unification as regards conceptuali-

---

[19] Cf. H. Birnbaum, "Balkanslavisch und Südslavisch: Zur Reichweite der Balkanismen im südslavischen Sprachraum", *Zeitschrift für Balkanologie* III (1965), 12-63, esp. 12-30 (with further references); *Idem*, "On Typology, Affinity, and Balkan Linguistics", *Zbornik za filologiju i lingvistiku* IX (1966), 17-30, esp. 17-19; *Idem*, "Slavjanskie jazyki na Balkanax i ponjatie tak nazyvaemyx jazykovyx sojuzov", *Glossa* 2: 1 (1968), 70-77.

zation and interpretation of reality as well as prevailing ideology; in assimilation and integration in terms of civilization (in the most general sense of the word) and technology, etc. (cf., for example, the loosely defined type of the West European or North-West European linguistic community[20] or even the trend toward typological-lexical integration increasingly welding certain partly only distantly related languages such as the particular Soviet brand of Modern Russian, 'East German', or Cuban Spanish together). The implications of utilizing deep structure properties (categories, relations) at this level or, to be more precise, within these differently defined typological layers for linguistic typology, thus supplementing, or perhaps even supplanting, traditional criteria for typological language classification with a new and more powerful set of linguistic parameters, will be discussed at some length in subsequent sections of this paper. Clearly, layers of deep structure defined in typological terms and characterized by properties going beyond one single language will command a higher degree of generality than the total of those encountered at the more 'shallow' level of 'infrastructure'.

(3) Finally, a stratum of greatest 'depth' and absolute generality, i.e., universality encompassing all (natural) languages or, rather, human language per se, as distinct from other semiotic systems of communication. For this deepest layer perhaps the term PROFOUND STRUCTURE could be reserved. While many deep structure features, ascertainable at less deep-seated strata (i.e., in 'shallow' and 'typological' deep structure) will be lost or, rather, irretrievable at this

---

[20] Cf., for example, J. Ellis, *Towards a General Comparative Linguistics* (The Hague, 1966), 142-153 ("Possible Comparisons of Balkan and North-West European Linguistic Community, with Reference to System-Reduction Method of Quantification"), esp. 144-148. See further also E. Lewy, "Der Bau der europäischen Sprachen", *Proceedings of the Royal Irish Academy* XLVIII, Section C (1942/3), 15-117, suggesting a division of the European languages into five geographico-typological groups (as represented by a total of eighteen particularly significant modern European languages). Lewy's five zones are as follows: 'Atlantic' (Basque, Spanish, French, Italian, Irish, English, Swedish); 'Central' (German, Hungarian); 'Balkan' (Albanian, Rumanian, Greek); 'Eastern' (Latvian, Russian, Finnish, Cheremiss, Mordvin); and 'Arctic' (Yurak, a Samoyed dialect).

deepest level, those properties identifiable at the profound or bottom layer must be characterized as truly universal and thus wholly invariant. It appears that perhaps most of deep structure in Chomsky's standard theory belongs precisely to this most generalized and universal level, which would also suggest that some of the deep structure categories and relations not retrievable or ascertainable at this level (and therefore used as an argument against the Chomskyan deep structure concept as such, e.g., by Lakoff) more properly belong to underlying, semantically based structures of less 'depth', accounted for under (1) and (2) above.

Since, then, we can roughly identify Chomsky's standard deep structure with what here has been termed 'profound structure' (disregarding, however, in this context the indeed fundamental difference of opinion as to its place and hence some essential facets of its function within an overall generative model of language, touched upon above), it may be appropriate to turn our attention primarily to the two other, less deep-seated strata of deep structure just singled out, that is, to shallow 'infrastructure' and to some further general characteristics of various typological deep structure layers.

First, some additional remarks on language-specific 'infrastructure'. It goes almost without saying that, being language-specific and, so to speak, closest to surface structure (to be sure, in its relatively most abstract state, i.e., syntactic and morphophonemic aspects), shallow 'infrastructure' will include all those properties and features which can find their surface expression in the syntactic synonymy of a given language or, in other words, in a complete set of possible, well-formed paraphrases of one and the same message (information-complex), without any semantic loss or addition. Of these deep-seated properties some will be limited to the 'infrastructure' level only while others will be represented at that level merely as reflections of categories and relations found at a deeper and hence more generalized level (typological or 'profound'), projected, as it were, into the 'shallow' level of deep structure. Such more deep-seated properties can thus belong to some typological deep structure underlying the surface (as well as the 'shallow') structure of a particular language as a result of the membership of that language in a typologically defined language group (genetic language family, linguistic convergence area, i.e., "Sprachbund", or otherwise); or they can be language-universal properties characteristic of all human language. It follows that the immediately underlying, shallow 'infrastructure' will be the richest and most varied, and, consequently, the least generalized of the deep structure layers ascertainable below the surface of any one language. Conversely, 'profound structure' (as defined above) will be the system most depleted of structural characteristics and relatively poorest as regards multiformity and diversity of semantically based categories and relations, and, as a consequence, the one with the maximal degree of generality (equaling universality) and invariance in terms of what can be regarded as specifically LINGUISTIC structure (as opposed to other conceivable systems of communication organized by some structural principle). However, this universality and invariance should not be confused with (structural) amorphousness, as is sometimes suggested or implied. As regards the deep dimension of language, it is thus only at the 'profound' level of semantics-related structure that we can gain any insight into the nature of language per se, while our better understanding of deep structure at the typological and 'shallow' levels could only help us to more adequately assess and characterize a particular language type (for details, see below) or an individual language. (Of course, this last statement refers only to the deep structure aspect of language, not to the transformational relationship obtaining between deep and surface structure, nor to the purely surface structure-related aspect of language with its own — phonological — universals.)

However, the relatively low degree of generality at the 'infrastructure' level should not be misinterpreted as having no generality to speak of. Having defined shallow 'infrastructure' as the abstract system immediately underlying the variable surface structures of syntactic synonymy (or of a complete set of grammatical paraphrases) in a given language, it should be clear that deep structure even at this 'shallow' level is generalized to a considerable extent.

At this point, to understand more fully the relationship between immediately underlying ('shallow') deep structures (here termed 'infrastructures') and their respective exponents in usually multiple surface structures (thus constituting paraphrases of each other), it may be useful to go back for a moment to the kind of transformational analysis preceding Chomsky's generative utilization of this device. I am referring to 'transformations' as elaborated in particular by Z. Harris (cf. references in fn. 4 above) and applied by him and others to resolve semantic ambiguities resisting, as it were, any further formal subclassification in terms of morphological and/or distributional criteria.[21] Here, then, the role of trans-

---

[21]   It should be noted that Chomsky seems to have applied for his own generative purposes the very transformation-device elaborated, to some extent, by Harris for refining an analytic (i.e., 'taxonomic') approach to linguistic structure. In this context it ought to be remembered, however, that neither was Harris the first to conceive of 'transformations' as an analytic device nor was Chomsky, by his own admission, the first to urge a generative view of language. As for the application of a transformational analysis of language for purposes of semantic classification beyond the overt one, readily observable in morphological and distributional categories, such an approach was suggested, to be sure, in a somewhat haphazard and perhaps not yet fully understood manner, for example by A. M. Peškovskij in his *Russkij sintaksis v naučnom osveščenii* (7th ed., Moscow, 1956); cf. 51 (fn. 1), 114 ff., 133 ff., 322, and elsewhere. A similar view was further expressed, among others, by E. Koschmieder in his essay "Die noetischen Grundlagen der Syntax" (originally presented in 1951 and first published in 1952). Thus, we read towards the end of this paper: "Für die syntaktischen Konstruktionen in den Wortverbindungen besteht der Nutzen der Noetik darin, dass der Untersucher das Zusammengehörige — auch wenn es formell geschieden ist — vereinen muss. Definiert man z. B. den Genetiv als Bedeutungsbereichseinschränkung, z. B. *domus patris*, so ist ersichtlich, dass *domus paterna* dasselbe meint und nun erhebt sich die Frage, ob Subst.[Subst.gen.] = Subst. Adj. ist, bzw. wie sie voneinander verschieden sind. Man wird die Frage aufwerfen müssen, ob es noch mehr gleichbedeutende Wortverbindungen gibt, wieweit man das eine für das andere setzen kann, und DIE UMFORMUNGS-REGELN DER SPRACHE ERGRÜNDEN MÜSSEN" (emphasis supplied; in: *Beiträge zur allgemeinen Syntax*, 88-89; in original version, 29, without the misprint "verneinen" for "vereinen"). Regarding Chomsky's predecessors in a transformational-generative approach to language, notably the Port Royal Grammar of 1660 and Humboldt (the latter, however, foreshadowed in his emphasis on the 'creative' aspect of language already by Descartes and his immediate followers), see Chomsky's own testimony, in particular, in his *Current Issues in Linguistic Theory*, 15-21, and *Cartesian Linguistics*, 3-31 ("Creative Aspect of Language Use", on Descartes and other rationalist thinkers down to Humboldt)

formations is reversed: whereas Chomsky's generative utilization of this device points up uniform deep structures underlying varying synonymous surface structures, Harris' transformational method serves to resolve homomorphous instances of polysemy. Thus, the respective directions of the transformational operations are, so to speak, opposite; but Harris' kind of analytic transformations may well contribute to elucidating the very relationship between surface structure and what here tentatively has been termed 'infrastructure' (or 'shallow deep structure'). Still, there is always a generative implication in any transformation: by separating homomorphous phrases or sentences on the basis of different meaning (lexical or nonlexical) we group each of these expressions with synonymous (or nearly synonymous) transforms, thus establishing a semantic relationship between them which, ultimately is based on deep structure identity.

A set of examples borrowed from Jakobson may serve here as an illustration.[22] In the following six Russian sentences the instrumental occurring in identical environments ('frames') carries six different contextual meanings (while, according to Jakobson, in all six instances the instrumental has a general meaning of marginality or peripheralness):

(1) *on el rebenkom ikru*   'he ate caviar as a child'
(2) *on el pudami ikru*   'he ate (the) caviar by the ton'
(3) *on el ložkoj ikru*   'he ate (the) caviar with a spoon'
(4) *on el dorogoj ikru*   'he ate (the) caviar on the way'
(5) *on el utrom ikru*   'he ate (the) caviar in the morning'
(6) *on el grešnym delom ikru* 'he ate (the) caviar, it's a shame to say'
                                             (or: '..., I'm sorry to say')

and 31-51 ("Deep and Surface Structure", as conceived in the Port Royal Grammar and by other rationalist, mostly French, grammarians). A method for morphological description essentially in generative ('predictive') terms was first suggested by R. Jakobson in his ground-breaking article "Russian Conjugation", *Word* 4, 155-167.

[22] Cf. R.O. Jakobson, in: *American Contributions to the Fourth International Congress of Slavicists, Moscow, September 1958* (The Hague, 1958), 130 (from his paper "Morfologičeskie nabljudenija nad slavjanskim skloneniem [Sostav russkix padežnyx form]").

Even if we have to allow for a considerable degree of adverbialization in several of the just quoted parallel sentences (viz., in (2), (4), and (5)) and for parenthetic interpolation in one, (6), the instrumental, though partly phraseologically petrified, is no doubt perceived as such by a native speaker of Russian in all six instances. Jakobson, therefore, uses these (and other) examples to illustrate his distinction (proposed in this as well as some other seminal papers) between contextual, syntactically and/or lexically conditioned variants, i.e., the 'extension' or actual application, of a case form, on the one hand, and, on the other, its general meaning, i.e., its 'intension', matching the morphological invariant (here, the instrumental form). While this distinction of general vs. specialized (contextual) meaning and a hierarchical patterning of general case meanings (and, for that matter, of general meanings of other morphological categories) can indeed contribute substantially to a more refined semantic interpretation of grammatical forms, the transformational approach, so convincingly applied at about the same time as Jakobson's Moscow congress paper (from which the above examples were taken) to precisely the Russian instrumental by D. S. Worth,[23] is bound to yield further and deeper insights into the semantic spectrum of particular grammatical forms, revealing a more complex functional-semantic structuredness not otherwise ascertainable, that is to say, not observable in the surface structure.[24]

---

[23] Cf. D. S. Worth, "Transform Analysis of Russian Instrumental Constructions", *Word* 14 (1958), 247-290 (available also in Russian translation: "Transformacionnyj analiz konstrukcij s tvoritel'nym padežom v russkom jazyke", in: *Novoe v lingvistike* II, V. A. Zvegincev [ed.] [Moscow, 1962], 637-683).

[24] Thus, example (1) above can be transformationally related to such synonymous or nearly synonymous sentences as: (1a) *kogda on byl rebenkom, on el ikru*; (1b) *buduči rebenkom, on el ikru*; (1c) *kak rebenok on el ikru*; (1d) *v detstve on el ikru*, etc. Likewise, example (3) can be paraphrased: (3a) *u nego byla ložka, kotoroj on el ikru*; (3b) *puskaja v xod ložku, on el ikru*; (3c) *ložka služila emu dlja edy ikry*; (3d) *on el ikru, nabiraja eë ložkoj*, etc. And, in a similar way, (6) can perhaps be rephrased, with more or less identical meaning, as: (6a) *on, grex skazat', el ikru*; (6b) *on, grešnyj čelovek, el ikru*; (6c) *on, k sožaleniju, el ikru*, etc. For one subfunction of the — grammatically unmarked — Russian infinitive, namely, its capability of serving as predicate in a sentence (thus replacing a finite verb form), a transformational approach was attempted by the present writer, allowing for a more refined subclassification of semantic

In this context it should be noted, however, that whereas, generally speaking, we can attempt to expound both the relative richness
and nonetheless considerable degree of generality of the immediately underlying 'shallow' level of deep structure by reference to surface
syntactic synonymy, transformationally exhibiting, as it were, the
abstract categories and relations of 'infrastructure', syntactic synonymy (i.e., a system of sets of grammatical paraphrases with identical semantic content) cannot, as noted by K. Gabka, be fully
equated with all 'transformational variants', as the latter may allow
for some, though usually fairly insignificant, loss and/or addition
of meaning.[25] On the other hand, it can be difficult at times to tell
whether a very slight semantic modification that may occur in
transformational paraphrasing necessarily reflects a difference in
properties (categories and/or configurations) even at the most
shallow level of deep structure. This is not the place, however,
to enter into a detailed discussion of these intricate problems;
rather, the preceding remarks were aimed at elucidating, if only
in a general and vague manner, the basic substance and extent of
'infrastructure', particularly in relation to the posited variable set
of intermediate layers of deep structure, here tentatively termed
'typological'.

---

shades and connotations expressed by the Russian infinitive within the general
meaning of predication; cf. H. Birnbaum, "Predication and the Russian Infinitive", *To Honor Roman Jakobson* I (The Hague, 1967), 271-294, esp. 287-
291 and 294. This paper is the slightly revised version of a chapter in a larger
monograph, *Studies on Predication in Russian* II: *On the Predicative Use of
the Russian Infinitive* (= Memorandum RM-4477-PR), (Santa Monica, Cal.,
The RAND Corp., 1965), (section 4, 104-141; cf. also section 3, "Some Transformations", 75-104, with further bibliography). For an earlier, pretransfor-
mational treatment of the overall functional range of the Russian infinitive,
see A.G.F. van Holk, *The Semantic Spectrum of the Russian Infinitive* (Leiden,
1953). Some other phenomena of Russian syntax approachable by a transformational-generative method were briefly sketched by R. Růžička in his outline *Studien zur Theorie der russischen Syntax*.
[25]   Cf. K. Gabka, "Zur Abgrenzung lexikalischer, morphologischer und syntaktischer Synonymie", *Zeitschrift für Slawistik* XII (1967), 727-734, esp. 728,
with ample further references particularly to literature treating syntactic
synonymy in Russian; in addition, see also V.P. Suxotin, *Sintaksičeskaja
sinonimika v sovremennom russkom literaturnom jazyke: Glagol'nye slovosočetanija* (Moscow, 1960).

3. TYPOLOGICAL DEEP STRUCTURE AND CATEGORY FUNCTION

It is probably not by sheer coincidence that the remarkable theory of language linked to the name of the author of "La stratification du langage" should be infused into the current American linguistic debate by the chief proponent of the trend known as 'stratificational grammar'.[26] The perceptiveness with which Sydney Lamb has scrutinized, modified, and in part incorporated some of the major tenets of Louis Hjelmslev's 'glossematics' into his own edifice of linguistic thought is undoubtedly more far-reaching than earlier as well as recent attempts to familiarize the American community of linguists with glossematic theory;[27] yet it seems that also Lamb in certain respects has perhaps not been able to grasp fully all the implications and consequences of Hjelmslev's concept of language. The impact made by the Danish linguist's theory on Wallace Chafe's view of linguistic structure was already briefly referred to above.[28]

In this context it is, on the other hand, interesting to note that glossematic theory is almost explicitly said to have contributed nothing to transformational generative grammar.[29] To be sure, the

[26] Cf. L. Hjelmslev, "La stratification du langage", reprinted in *Essais linguistiques*, 36-68 (for full reference, see nn. 7 and 8, above); see further S. M. Lamb, "Epilegomena to a Theory of Language", *Romance Philology* XIX (1966), 531-573. For a preliminary presentation of 'stratificational grammar', see *Idem, Outline of Stratificational Grammar* (Washington, D. C., 1966); Lamb's approach to semantics is now also sketched in his brief survey "Lexicology and Semantics", in: *Linguistics Today*, A. A. Hill (ed.) (New York–London, 1969), 40-49.

[27] E. Haugen, in his paper "Directions in Modern Linguistics", *Language* 27 (1951), 211-222, and P. L. Garvin, in his review of Hjelmslev's *Prolegomena*, *Language* 30 (1954), 69-96, were instrumental in primarily translating the basic glossematic terminology and conceptual framework into a set of postulates and notions more readily accessible to an essentially neo-Bloomfieldian, i.e., behavioristically slanted, host of linguists. Of more recent introductions, cf., in particular, F. Whitfield's "Glossematics", in: *Linguistics Today*, 250-258.

[28] Cf. Chafe's article referred to above (n. 10); the impact of Hjelmslevian linguistics is also strongly felt in his *Explorations in the Theory of Language* (forthcoming).

[29] Only scarce reference to glossematic theory can be found in Chomsky's prolific writing on theoretical linguistics. Where such reference occurs it is,

fundamental outlook of Hjelmslev's and Chomsky's respective approaches to language differ substantially. Though highly abstract, linguistic 'form', the primary object of a structural linguistics as Hjelmslev conceived of it, must be thought of as something given beforehand or, rather, as an abstract structure underlying something given, viz., the linguistic data, in other words, as *ergon*. As has been stated over and over again, for the adherents of generative grammar, on the other hand, a 'taxonomic' description and analysis aiming at classification and/or segmentation of linguistic data is as such both inadequate and trivial. It is perfectly true, therefore, that nothing in Chomsky's and his followers' views on the nature of language can in any way be directly traced back to, or even vaguely identified with, anything specifically contained in Hjelmslev's major theoretical writings, above all his *Prolegomena to a Theory of Language*. However, this does not necessarily apply to some of the ideas loosely sketched in Hjelmslev's booklet *Sproget* (available also in a French translation; an English version is in press) which, although drafted at approximately the same time as his *magnum opus* (i.e., the Danish original, *Omkring sprogteoriens grundlæggelse*, published in 1943), was to become his last major scholarly contribution.[30] Needless to say, no direct influence of Hjelmslev on Chomsky can be assumed here either, let alone ascertained. While couched in a style readily accessible to a broad public, the Danish linguist's last book can in many ways be considered a companion volume to the earlier theoretical work. This time the focus of attention is on the previously almost overlooked aspects of genetic and typological linguistics.

Specifically, Hjelmslev defines genetic relationship between lan-

---

as a rule, in negative and dissociating terms; cf., e.g., N. Chomsky, *Syntactic Structures* (3rd printing), (The Hague, 1963), 50 (fn. 1); *Idem, Current Issues in Linguistic Theory*, 75 (fn. 13).

[30] Cf. L. Hjelmslev, *Sproget: En introduktion* (Copenhagen, 1963); French version: *Le langage: Une introduction* (translated by M. Olsen, with a preface by A.J. Greimas), (Paris, 1966). The English translation, now in press, was prepared by F.J. Whitfield.

guages as a 'function'[31] obtaining between languages where each 'expression element', that is roughly, each phonological segment or its graphic manifestion, of one language is correlated with that of another language with each such element being conditioned by its environment and its position within the word. This determination of genetic relationship between languages is said to be an OPERATIONAL definition providing a criterion for determining whether, in a given instance, there is genetic relationship or not. While the very nature of the 'function' correlating the 'expression elements' of different — closely or remotely related — languages is, to begin with, not further examined, it can nonetheless be labeled a CONTINUATION, implying that each 'expression element' of any one language CONTINUES the common formulae and that, consequently, each genetically related language continues the total system of common formulae.[32] Thus, genetic relationship is viewed by Hjelmslev as establishable on the basis of continuity and differentiation of the expression plane of language in terms of a system of phonological correspondences. The common formulae of 'expression elements' suggest such elements as reconstructable or attested in the phonological structures of protolanguages from which the genetically related languages have developed; and the total system of common formulae corresponds by and large to the overall expression plane (or phonological structure) of one

---

[31] 'Function' in glossematic usage is defined as 'dependence that fulfills the conditions for an analysis' and 'analysis', in turn, is said to be a 'description of an object by the uniform dependences of other objects on it and on each other'. In less technical language, therefore, 'function' can be rendered by 'dependence', which is either a 'dependence relation', if obtaining between parts of a 'chain' ('text'; 'both-and function'), or a 'dependence correlation', if obtaining between members of a 'paradigm' ('language'; 'either-or function'). The terminals of a 'function', i.e., the objects that have 'function' to other objects, are in glossematic terminology referred to as 'functives'. Cf. L. Hjelmslev, *Prolegomena*, 131-132 and 134-135 (definitions 1, 2, 8, 9, 10, 26, 27, 54, 56, and 57).

[32] Cf. for a more detailed account for the essence of genetic relationship between languages, as here summarized, L. Hjelmslev, *Le langage*, 31-54, esp. 34 (for a definition of 'expression element') and 52-53 (for a general definition of genetic linguistic relationship); in the Danish original, the corresponding references are 14-34, esp. 16-17 and 33.

particular protolanguage. Needless to say, this would apply only
to the stock of words inherited from a common parent language
while in other cases, particularly of lexical borrowing, common
formulae of 'expression elements' could, where applicable, at best
refer to a theoretical ('potential') word form of which the various
actually existing shapes of loan and foreign words might be considered phonological adaptations.

By contrast, though in a parallel way, typological relationship
between languages can be defined, according to Hjelmslev, as a
'function' obtaining between languages, where certain 'categories'
found in each of a group of languages may be correlated with a
set of corresponding 'categories' in the other languages of that
group. Thus, as genetic relationship is revealed by '(expression)
element function' between languages, typological relationship (occasionally also referred to as linguistic 'affinity') can be shown to
exist on the basis of what Hjelmslev termed 'category function',
discounting, in this context, the purely external and most fortuitous
aspects of linguistic structure, viz., word structure. Among 'categories', Hjelmslev distinguished between those of linguistic 'schema'
(or 'structure'): thus, in the expression plane, for example, vowels
and consonants, various prosodic entities (with further subcate-
gorization); in the content plane, grammatical categories, such as
case, gender, number, etc.; and, on the other hand, those of linguistic 'usage': in the expression plane, for example, sound categories; in the content plane, various semantic categories ('features').[33]

It is certainly not my intention to deny that category correlations
ascertainable in the expression plane of various languages, whether
they be assigned to the 'linguistic schema' or to 'linguistic usage',

---

[33] Cf. L. Hjelmslev, *Le language*, 123-129, esp. 127-128 (in the Danish original,
88-93, esp. 92). 'Category' was defined by Hjelmslev as a "paradigmatic sum",
i.e., "a paradigm that has correlation to one or more other paradigms within
the same rank"; cf. *Prolegomena*, 84-85 and 135-136 (definition 75, with further
references). On the terms 'linguistic schema' (or 'structure') and 'linguistic
usage', related to, though not identical with, both Saussure's *langue/parole*
dichotomy and Chomsky's 'competence' vs. 'performance' distinction, see, in
particular, *Prolegomena*, 75-81, and further also Hjelmslev's 1943 article
"Langue et parole", reprinted in *Essais linguistiques*, 69-81.

can provide a basis for typological grouping of languages. Indeed, to take a well-known example, Jakobson's early work on phonological convergence areas (*phonologische Sprachbünde, affinités* or *unions phonologiques*) was aimed at demonstrating phonological traits — say, polytony vs. monotony, presence vs. absence of palatal or palatalized sounds (as contrasted with nonpalatal or nonpalatalized sounds), syllabic synharmony or suprasyllabic vowel harmony, etc. — as criteria for linguistic typology, yielding broadly conceived, 'extensive' linguistic convergence areas (such as, for example, an alleged 'Eurasian' or a 'Baltic-North European' *Sprachbund*).[34] Nonetheless, it appears that it is the categories of the content plane, that is, the semantically based 'categories' of 'linguistic schema' and 'usage', that can provide the most powerful tool for language typology. It is, then, these categories (and their syntagmatic configurations, where, however, we do not have to conceive of 'syntagmatic relationships' or 'configurations' as originally sequentially ordered) that seem to make up, essentially, what here has

---

[34]   Cf. R. Jakobson, *Selected Writings* I (The Hague, 1962), 137-201, 234-246, and, for a self-critical retrospect, 651-652. For some reservations and further references (also to some related publications by N. S. Trubeckoj, a fellow-'Eurasian'), see H. Birnbaum, *Zeitschrift für Balkanologie* III (1965), 12 (fn. 1) and 14-16 (with fnn. 4 and 5). Further examples of 'phonological integration' or 'typologization' could be provided, for example, by Italian and Serbo-Croatian (and, perhaps, Albanian, thus forming, as it were, an 'Adriatic phonological convergence area') or by Rumanian and Slavic, especially Bulgarian. On the latter problem, cf., in particular, E. Petrovici, *Kann das Phonemsystem einer Sprache durch fremden Einfluss umgestaltet werden? Zum slavischen Einfluss auf das rumänische Lautsystem* (The Hague, 1957). Another case in point could be furnished by newly established standard Moldavian, based essentially on a set of Daco-Rumanian dialects but strongly influenced by Slavic, primarily Ukrainian and Russian, phonology (as reflected also in the use of the Cyrillic alphabet). For a recent attempt to delineate the Balkan linguistic convergence area in terms of its phonological integration, see E. A. Afendras, *The Balkans as a Linguistic Area: A Study in Phonological Convergence* (unpublished doctoral dissertation, The Johns Hopkins University, 1968). Generally on the *Sprachbund* phenomenon, see, of more recent contributions, E. Seidel, "Zur Problematik des Sprachbundes", in: *Beiträge zur Sprachwissenschaft, Volkskunde und Literaturforschung: W. Steinitz zum 60. Geburtstag...*, (Berlin, 1965), 372-381; and V. Georgiev, "Le problème de l'union linguistique balkanique", *Actes du Premier Congrès international des études balkaniques et sud-est européennes* VI (Sofia, 1968), 7-19.

been isolated and identified as the typological strata of (fundamentally, Chomskyan) deep structure.[35]

In this context, the importance of COVERT CATEGORIES, recently pointed out by C.J. Fillmore, deserves particular attention. According to Fillmore, "many recent and not-so-recent studies have convinced us of the relevance of grammatical properties lacking obvious 'morphemic' realizations but having a reality that can be observed on the basis of selectional constraints and TRANSFORMATIONAL POSSIBILITIES. We are constantly finding that GRAMMATICAL FEATURES found in one language SHOW UP IN SOME FORM OR OTHER IN OTHER LANGUAGES as well, if we have the subtlety it takes to DISCOVER COVERT CATEGORIES" (emphasis added).[36] However, I cannot, for reasons that by now should be obvious, entirely follow Fillmore when he goes on claiming that the concept 'covert category' is "a concept which is making it possible to believe that AT BOTTOM all languages are essentially alike" (emphasis supplied).[37] To be sure, also in my view, SOME of the 'covert categories' may well belong or, rather, no doubt belong to the 'profound structure' of language, as defined above, thus indeed being language-universal. But other such categories may very well belong to one or another of the typological deep structure strata of language, that is to say, be ascertainable only in the deep structure of certain — typologically related — languages, but not in all human language. Notice, however, that this is not tantamount to saying that, from a structural viewpoint, not ALL categories expressable, by grammatical (nonlexical) or lexical means, in one language can be rendered also, nonlexically or lexically, in any other language. Yet if no one-to-one relationship of 'covert categories' can be established

---

[35] For some previous juxtapositions, if not identifications, of (a part of) Hjelmslev's 'category function' with (a segment of) Chomsky's deep structure, see my pertinent remarks in *Zbornik za filologiju i lingvistiku* IX (1966), 18 (with fn. 4); *Studies in Slavic Linguistics and Poetics in Honor of Boris O. Unbegaun*, 28 (fn. 4); *American Contributions to the Sixth International Congress of Slavists*, Vol. I: *Linguistic Contributions*, 52 (fn. 48); *Folia Linguistica* II (1969), 7 (with fnn. 8 and 9). See also p. 78, below.

[36] The quotation is from *Universals in Linguistic Theory*, 3.

[37] *Ibid.* Cf., however, also Fillmore's interesting remarks on language typology, *op. cit.*, 51-60.

between two languages, any 'translating' of one such category into another category or, rather, into an arbitrary, unpredictable categorial subset (i.e., a segment of one category or any combination of two or more, complete or partial categories, as the case may be) of another language implies a contrasting of two languages with fundamentally different deep-structural articulations. Such languages must therefore be considered typologically unrelated (in their respective semantic or content aspects). In other words, typological relationship between languages can, even in its broadest application, not be reduced to a relationship which can be expressed in terms of universals inherent in all natural languages. On the other hand, it is only on the basis of identifying deep-seated properties recurrent in all language types that we are able to establish an even 'deeper' set of categories ascertainable at the universal 'profound structure' level of language.

Thus, while we roughly identify the categories of the content plane entering into content-based 'category function' in Hjelmslev's sense with the 'covert categories' of the intermediate, typological strata of deep structure (essentially in Chomsky's sense), it seems important to point out that, in my opinion, Hjelmslev's strict distinction between genetic and typological relationship is valid only to a limited extent. For, put in somewhat oversimplified terms, it could be said that while genetic relationship between languages can be revealed only on the basis of '(expression) element function' (to use Hjelmslev's term), i.e., on the basis of phonological — and, secondarily, graphic — correspondences, traceable to underlying 'common formulae' (which in most instances is tantamount to saying: to 'expression elements' of historically preceding protolanguages), such a genetic relationship implies also some degree of typological relationship, since genetically related languages, in addition to exhibiting symbolization correlations, also share a greater or lesser number of common or, rather, correlatable structural properties at a (typological) deep structure level. To be sure, the simultaneous membership of a language in several typological groupings may entail a partial replacement of typological properties originally characteristic of a genetically closely related language group by other properties peculiar to a group of genetically unrelated or only remotely related languages of which the given language also is a member. But if recognizable as a member of a particular genetically related language group, that language will always retain a greater or lesser number of semantically based features ('covert categories') that can be identified only with that language family. To take an example, it could be said that Bulgarian, being both a (South) Slavic and a Balkan language, is characterized by fewer deep-seated properties peculiar of the Slavic language TYPE than, say, Polish or Russian, some of them having been superseded by typical Balkan linguistic features ('Balkanisms'); nonetheless, Bulgarian can no doubt be shown to be also a Slavic language on the basis of typological deep-seated properties even if such properties here will be somewhat less numerous than in the two other Slavic languages mentioned. In addition, the Slavic character of Bulgarian can be demonstrated, of course, by means of the exclusively genetic criterion, viz., 'expression element function' with other Slavic languages. Thus, a typological approach also to genetically related languages must certainly be considered legitimate.[38]

---

[38] Many attempts to characterize the Slavic language family in typological terms, thus singling it out from among other (non-Slavic) languages but also contrasting individual Slavic languages with each other, have been undertaken, particularly in recent years. Cf., for example, for a 'phonological typology', M.I. Lekomceva, D.M. Segal, T.M. Sudnik, S.M. Šur, "Opyt postroenija fonologičeskoj tipologii blizkorodstvennyx jazykov", in: *Slavjanskoe jazykoznanie. Doklady sovetskoj delegacii. V Meždunarodnyj s'ezd slavistov (Sofija, sentjabr' 1963)* (Moscow, 1963), 423-476; and for a 'morphological typology', Z.M. Volockaja, T.N. Mološnaja, T.M. Nikolaeva, I.I. Revzin, T.V. Civ'jan, "Ob odnom podxode k tipologii slavjanskix jazykov (na materiale sistemy sklonenija suščestvitel'nogo)", *ibid.*, 510-552 (with ample references to previous studies in Slavic typology). A generative framework of language modeling for a typological description of the Slavic languages is sketched in I.I. Revzin, *Metod modelirovanija i tipologija slavjanskix jazykov* (Moscow, 1967). For another attempt at a typological characterization of the Slavic linguistic group, this time focusing on syntax, particularly crucial for deep structure, see R. Růžička, "Zur syntaktischen Typologie moderner slawischer Literatursprachen", *Zeitschrift für Slawistik* VIII (1963), 833-860. Obviously, a typological-contrastive syntactic analysis of a well-established language family such as the Slavic (implying also typological relationship) must focus

The realization that we can posit a typological deep structure layer underlying also genetically related languages — even a more loosely related group such as the Indo-European languages as a whole — may provide us with further important insights as to some general characteristics and tendencies of Indo-European syntax. It can also shed some new light on the occasionally claimed high susceptibility of the syntax of one language (as compared to other components of the structure of that language) to influences from syntactic models and patterns of other, likewise Indo-European languages. Discussing recently some aspects of loan syntax in Slavic in general and in Old Church Slavic in particular, I arrived at the conclusion that "as applied to a set of genetically related natural languages, one could, for example, venture to say that much of the deep structure underlying the surface data of most, if not all, of the recorded ancient Indo-European languages displays a considerable degree of uniformity, thus suggesting a new, promising approach to the problem of reconstructing Proto-Indo-European syntax." Superficially seen, syntax has correctly been assigned a high degree of 'penetrability' (by comparison with phonology and morphology). It can, however, in its typological deep structure

---

both on shared structural features, establishing the typological relationship, and on internal deviations, caused, among other things, by contacts with various other languages. Thus, Růžička (as well as others) could show that some of the differences in syntactic structure between Contemporary Standard Russian and Modern Czech are due, in large part, to the impact made by the Old Church Slavic-Greek tradition and French, on the one hand, and by Latin and German, on the other; cf. also H. Birnbaum, *Studies in Slavic Linguistics and Poetics in Honor of Boris O. Unbegaun*, 27 and 31 (fnn. 21-23). Cf. now further also R. Mrázek, "Dedukce a empirie při srovnávací typologii slovanské věty", in: *Otázky slovanské syntaxe*, II *Sborník symposia "Strukturní typy slovanské věty a jejich vývoj"*, *Brno 20.-22. X. 1966* (Brno, 1968), 185-200. — Much more complicated is the problem when syntactic criteria are applied to reveal assumed genetic relationship between languages where such a relationship has not been previously ascertained or where, at any rate, it is highly controversial. Here syntactic correspondences are more apt to indicate a typological relationship which may or may not be genetic as well. For an interesting attempt of that kind, claiming syntactic data for establishing genetic relationship between the Uralic and Altaic language families (accepted by some linguists, but rejected by others), see D. R. Fokos-Fuchs, *Rolle der Syntax in der Frage nach der Sprachverwandtschaft mit besonderer Rücksicht auf das Problem der ural-altaischen Sprachverwandtschaft* (Wiesbaden, 1962).

aspect, "actually be considered a fairly stable component of language also when viewed in the context of bilingualism and language interference."[39]

To illustrate the above considerations by at least one example, reference can be made here to the so-called absolute case constructions, equivalent to subordinate clauses, as encountered in several Indo-European languages, particularly in their early stages of attestation. Thus, as is well known, to the classical (and Byzantine) Greek genitive absolute construction corresponds in Latin the *ablativus absolutus* while Old Church Slavic and, as it seems, largely under the influence of Old Church Slavic, some other Slavic languages have an equivalent dative absolute construction, to which counterparts can be found, incidentally, also in Gothic and Lithuanian, the latter a highly archaic modern representative of the Indo-European language family. And even such phrases as contemporary English *God willing, weather permitting,* or *decision pending* (= 'if God will', 'if weather permits', 'while a/the decision is pending') might, perhaps, be interpreted as residues of an older Germanic absolute case construction (with the original case form having been obliterated in Modern English). To be sure, the relationships between some of these Indo-European absolute case phrases remain controversial, notably those of Greek and Old Church Slavic and, similarly, those of Greek and Gothic, but also, for example, those of Slavic (Old Russian, Early Belorussian, to a lesser extent Early Ukrainian) and Lithuanian, with some scholars even claiming — erroneously, in my opinion — an altogether mechanical and artificial construction-transfer from one language to another (e.g., from Greek to Old Church Slavic or from Lithuanian to Early Belorussian).[40] Yet much seems to point here to an

---

[39] Cf. H. Birnbaum, "On Deep Structure and Loan Syntax in Slavic", *Studies in Slavic Linguistics and Poetics in Honor of Boris O. Unbegaun*, 21-31, esp. 22-23; for further exemplification (from Greek and Old Church Slavic) and elaboration of this viewpoint, see also my Prague congress paper, "Obščeslavjanskoe nasledie i inojazyčnye obrazcy v strukturnyx raznovidnostjax staroslavjanskogo predloženija", quoted above.

[40] Gothic, in addition to a fairly frequent dative absolute construction, assumed to be largely patterned after the Greek *genitivus absolutus* (example: *miþ-*

underlying Common Indo-European 'covert category' (i.e., a semantically based category at the 'Indo-European typological deep structure level'), containing, along with some other components, such semantic features as [+PREDICATION] and [+SUBORDINATION] which, at the surface level, found its

---

weitwodjandein mis miþwissein meinai = συμμαρτυρούσης μοι τῆς συνειδήσεώς μου, Rom. 9, 1), occasionally uses a nominative absolute (example: *jah waurþans dags gatils* = καὶ γενομένης ἡμέρας εὐκαίρου, Mc. 6, 21) as well as an accusative absolute phrase (example: *Jah atgaggandein inn dauhtar Herodiadins* = καὶ εἰσελθούσης τῆς θυγατρὸς αὐτῆς τῆς Ἡρῳδιάδος, Mc. 6, 22); for details, further examples, and some explanations of the controversial origin of these constructions, see W. Krause, *Handbuch des Gotischen*³ (Munich, 1968), 140 (§ 114, 2), 144-145 (§§ 116, 9 and 117, 2). In Lithuanian, a noun or pronoun in the dative combines frequently with an uninflected gerund (the gerund having developed from an original participle) to replace a subordinate clause (example: *mán važiúojant* 'while I was travelling'); if the expression is impersonal or the subject thought of as indefinite, the gerund alone (i.e., without a dative 'subject') may be used (example: *reĩkiant* 'if [it is] necessary'). Cf. further, with additional examples, A. Senn, *Handbuch der litauischen Sprache*, Bd. I: *Grammatik* (Heidelberg, 1966), 474-475 (§ 1115); on the use of the dative absolute in Old Lithuanian, see also the special study by V. Ambrazas, "Absoliutinis naudininkas XVI-XVIIa. lietuvių kalbos paninkluose", *Lietuvių kalbotyros klausimai* 5 (1962), 56-80. For references to the conflicting opinions regarding the Old Church Slavic dative absolute phrases, including impersonal constructions with merely a participle in the dative (examples: *mьnogo sǫštu narodu* = πολλοῦ ὄχλου ὄντος, Mc. 8, 1; *pozdě sǫštu* 'as it was late'; exceptionally also a genitive absolute, imitating the Greek original, e.g., *nikogo že sǫšta učitelja* = μηδενὸς ὄντος διδασκάλου, Supr. 415, 1) see my remarks in *American Contributions to the Sixth International Congress of Slavists*, Vol. I: *Linguistic Contributions*, 39-40 (with fn. 28), 48-49 (with fnn. 43 and 44), 57-60 (with fnn. 61-65). For further details on the occurrences of the dative absolute in East Slavic, including instances of combinations of dative 'subjects' with uninflected gerunds, stemming historically from active participles (examples: Old Russian *priěxavšimъ imъ* 'when they had arrived', Hyp. Chr., 204a; *Izjaslavu že xotjašču poiti ko Kievu* 'and as Izjaslav wanted [or: was about] to march to Kiev', *ibid.*, 175b; Early Belorussian *suščju[ž] emu u Němcaxъ u Marъině gradě* '[and] while he was in Germany at Marienburg', Acad. Chr., 178a; with gerund: *buduči nam v Kovne* 'being in Kaunas, [we...]; as we were in Kaunas...', Kaunas County Court Records of 1566/7, 42b), with some comments also on the possible influence of Lithuanian, particularly on the spreading of this phenomenon in Early Belorussian documents beyond the realm of the 'bookish' (i.e., Church Slavic-influenced) language and on some residual occurrences in contemporary dialects as well as in spoken Belorussian, see now in particular the chapter on the dative absolute (authored by E.I. Kedajtene) in *Sravnitel'no-istoričeskij sintaksis vostočnoslavjanskix jazykov: Členy predloženija*, V.I. Borkovskij (ed.), (Moscow, 1968), 275-286,

expression, wherever possible, in a particular case form (used 'absolutely') of a noun or pronoun (corresponding to the subject of a two-membered clause with a finite verb form, i.e., expressing the feature [+ AGENT]) and an agreeing participle (or uninflected gerund; corresponding to the predicate of a two-membered clause, i.e., expressing the feature [±ACTION]). The particular choice of case in languages having a well-defined formal case system (genitive, ablative, dative), determined by an interplay of semantic and morphological factors, is secondary and language-specific compared to the more general characteristic of Indo-European of availing itself of participial (and subsequently gerundial) constructions in an 'absolute' case to express a predicative-subordinate function or meaning.[41]

---

with numerous references to the relevant literature. Most recently the problem of the dative absolute constructions in Baltic and Slavic has been tackled by H. Andersen in a thought-provoking paper, "The Dative of Subordination in Baltic and Slavic", *Baltic Linguistics*, T. F. Magner, W. R. Schmalstieg (eds.) (University Park and London, 1970), 1—9. While I cannot quite agree with Andersen when he entirely rules out any influence whatsoever of Greek on the rise — or, as I would prefer to put it, activation — of the dative absolute construction in (Old) Church Slavic, his monogenetic theory, favored over a polygenetic view, to explain the origin of the absolute case constructions in various Indo-European languages as well as his arguments, largely along Jakobsonian lines of semantic reasoning, justifying the choice of the dative in Baltic and Slavic (as well as Gothic, representing Germanic at large) are, in my view, indeed fully convincing (cf. also the quotation in the following note).
[41] Cf. the following statement by H. Andersen, *loc. cit.*, 3—4. closely approximating my own view as set forth in the present paper: "In reconstructing absolute constructions as part of Proto-Indo-European syntax one has to abstract from two sets of facts concerning the attested languages. — In the first place, it is clear that the development of participial systems belongs to the history of the individual Indo-European dialects. But it is essential to recognize that the development of these morphological categories is distinct from the existence of a syntactic pattern, a set of transformational rules which produced absolute constructions, i.e., sentences containing a participle instead of a finite verb form. The fact that these transformational rules in the various languages where they are found operate with different participles is a function of the diversity of the participial systems and has no direct bearing on the reconstruction of the Proto-Indo-European absolute construction. This latter problem in comparative Indo-European syntax must be solved on the basis of a comparison of syntactic rules, not of systems of participles. — The second set of facts that has to be abstracted from is the use of different cases in the absolute constructions of the different languages, the ablative in Latin, the

For a segment of a different area of typological-contrastive study based on the deep structure concept, namely, that of Latin, the Romance languages, especially Spanish, and English (with some excursions also into the field of Greek-Latin syntactic borrowing), reference can now be made to the recent findings of R.T. Lakoff which, to a considerable extent, seem to corroborate the basic view taken here with regard to the relative stability of Indo-European deep structure in contradistinction to the observable superficial disparity among various individual representatives of that language family.[42] In particular, Lakoff has found that for a part of the grammar of Latin the syntactic rules for postulating deep structures are, in fact, similar to those of English. In other words, Latin and English are shown not to differ greatly in their complement systems regardless of their apparent surface-structural differences. Moreover, Lakoff has been able to demonstrate, among other things, that, if viewed in the abstract, negatives behave by and large similarly in Latin and in English and also that the superficial difference between single and double negatives in Latin and Spanish, respectively, can be reduced to a uniform model at the deep structure level.

Considerations of space prevent any further references to recent and current work in the field of transformational-generative Indo-European syntax or semantics (in the broad sense, as reinterpreted

---

genitive in Greek, the locative and genitive in Sanskrit, the dative in Baltic, Slavic, and Germanic. This diversity has by many scholars been taken as evidence that absolute constructions arose independently in the various Indo-European languages, but this inference is unwarranted. It is perfectly possible to suppose that case usage in the absolute construction can have changed in the individual Indo-European dialects as their respective case systems evolved. Indeed one must allow for this possibility if one assumes that a case system is not a mere inventory of forms, but a coherent system of grammatical meanings. What this means is that although there are sufficient grounds for positing for Proto-Indo-European a set of syntactic rules which produced absolute constructions, we should not try to determine which case was originally used in these constructions."

[42] See R.T. Lakoff, *Abstract Syntax and Latin Complementation* (*M.I.T. Research Monograph* 49) (Cambridge, Mass., 1968).

above).[43] May it suffice, therefore, to state here that, in my view,
as we can, and indeed must, posit a typological deep structure
stratum for closely related languages such as the Slavic or the
Romance, a 'deeper', i.e., more generalized and hence less rich and
more simplified, deep structure layer ought also to be postulated
for the Indo-European linguistic type. The same is true, of course,
also of the other major phylogenetic language groups of the world.

To sum up, then, the substance of the preceding argumentation:
Whereas 'infrastructure' can be defined as the language-specific
shallow deep structure immediately underlying the surface structure of any one given language, finding its transformationally
derived expression in the syntactic synonymy of that particular
language, and whereas, on the other hand, 'profound structure',
at the 'bottom' of stratified deep structure, can be viewed as the
language-universal layer of that structure characteristic of all language (thus differentiating natural language as such from other
semiotic and communicative systems), the several intermediate
layers of deep structure where the abstract properties ('covert
categories') of phylogenetically or otherwise structurally related
languages are based may be more difficult to identify and to clearly single out. Yet as larger or smaller groups of languages are
characterized by similar or, rather, one-to-one-correlated features
and categories in the surface structure, these superficial characteristics can be transformationally derived from and ultimately
reduced to abstract deep-seated categories and relations which,
while contained or, to be precise, reflected also in the 'infrastructure' of each individual member language of that group, cannot,
on the other hand, be traced back to properties of such profound
'depth' that they could be said to be universal and of utmost
generality and thus found to underlie, in the last analysis, the surface structures of all languages. Any language group that can be
reasonably said to be held together by a significant number of
shared or matching structural features will be considered to constitute a language TYPE. From a synchronic viewpoint and in terms

[43] In particular, some recent studies, published and unpublished, by P.
Kiparsky seem to deserve attention in this context.

of the deep structure aspect it is of secondary import whether the languages making up a particular language type are genetically related, i.e., go back to a common protolanguage (recorded or reconstructed), or whether their typological relationship is due to other — external — circumstances such as symbiosis, geographical proximity, cultural integration, sub- or superstratum leveling, or the like. However, it should be noted that, with few exceptions, only genetically related languages will generally exhibit shared or even correlatable structural features also in the expression plane, i.e., primarily sound correspondences (but cf., for example, the effect of Slavic on the phonological system of Rumanian, referred to in note 34). At least when it comes to the semantic aspect of linguistic structure, including deep structure, genetic relationship between languages can, therefore, be considered but a particular instance of the broader notion of typological relationship, the former always implying the latter, but not necessarily vice versa.

4. TYPOLOGICAL DEEP STRUCTURE AND METALINGUISTIC MODELING: THE BALKAN CONVERGENCE AREA

Even if genetically related language families can thus, in their deep structure aspect, be conceived of as merely forming a subclass of the overall class of typological language groups, it is on typological groupings in the traditional and narrow sense, i.e., as referring to language groups displaying a sizable number of structural agreements and conformities and comprising genetically unrelated or perhaps only remotely related languages (along with, optionally, some closely related languages as well), that this new deep structure-oriented approach to linguistic typology primarily ought to be tested. The classical example of a structurally integrated linguistic convergence area, viz., that of the Balkan languages proper (sharing a number of common 'Balkanisms'), seems to provide an ideal testing ground.[44] Indeed, considerable work along lines, sim-

[44] For a recent definition of the Balkan LINGUISTIC convergence area, in particular as it ought to be delineated in relation to some other languages of the Southeast European GEOGRAPHIC area, see my remarks in *Zeitschrift für*

ilar to those briefly sketched above, has already been accomplished. In a study on the methods of structural linguistic typology, the Soviet linguist B.A. Uspenskij, a former student of Hjelmslev's, has amplified, and to some degree formalized, some of the ideas loosely and in an informal fashion outlined by the great Danish scholar.[45] In his study, available now also in English translation, Uspenskij introduces the notion of a METALINGUISTIC MODEL (or 'étalon language', Russian *jazyk-ètalon*) as a tool for typological language confrontation.[46] Such a metalanguage is defined as an ABSTRACT model which is used as a standard in contrastive language analysis on one or several levels of grammar (in the broad sense). It is suggested that the degree of typological resemblance between languages be measured in terms of their respective proximity to or, conversely, deviational distance from this adopted metalinguistic model. The degree of proximity or deviation to be used as a typological index can be stated by means of a set of transformational rules mapping the semantically interpreted deep structure (or a fragment thereof) underlying a given natural language onto phonologically interpreted surface structures and correlating the discovered deep structure with the generalized structure or sub-

---

Balkanologie III (1965), 18-30 ("Balkanischer Sprachbund und südosteuropäischer Sprachraum").

[45] The following paraphrases slightly, with some omissions and additions, my previous discussion of Uspenskij's new methodology and, subsequently, of T.V. Civ'jan's application of fundamentally this approach to Balkan linguistics (cf. note 50 below), as it appeared in *Zbornik za filologiju i lingvistiku* IX (1966), 19-25, and *Folia Linguistica* II (1969), 8-13 (with further references), reprinted pp. 80-85, below. Cf. also my review of Civ'jan's book in *Zeitschrift für Balkanologie* IV (1966), 173-181.

[46] Cf. B.A. Uspenskij, *Strukturnaja tipologija jazykov* (Moscow, 1965), esp. 58-68 ("Tipologija i jazyk-ètalon") and, for English summary, 241-242; see now also the English translation of Uspenskij's earlier book *Principy strukturnoj tipologii* (Moscow, 1962): B. Uspenskij, *Principles of Structural Typology* (The Hague–Paris, 1968). The theoretical aspects of basing typological language classification on the concept of a metalinguistic model were explored by Uspenskij in an earlier paper, "Tipologičeskaja klassifikacija jazykov kak osnova jazykovyx sootvetstvij (Struktura jazyka-ètalona pri tipologičeskoj klassifikacii jazykov)", *Voprosy jazykoznanija* 6 (1961), 51-64. On the impact of glossematic theory on Uspenskij, cf. also his impressions reported in "Lingvističeskaja žizn' Kopengagena", *Voprosy jazykoznanija* 3 (1962), 148-151.

structure (rather than 'amorphous structure', suggested by Uspenskij) of the abstract 'étalon language'. As follows from this reasoning, deep structure (of a particular language) is here conceived of as an organized system underlying a specific LANGUAGE TYPE (to be further defined) rather than underlying language per se, i.e., all language. In other words, deep structure in this context carries primarily typological connotations while the deep-seated language-specific deviations to be measured against the abstract, ideal typological metalinguistic model would seem to belong to that layer of underlying, semantically based structure that here has tentatively been termed 'infrastructure'. Put somewhat differently, one could therefore venture to say that Uspenskij's typological measurements can be expressed in terms of contrasting the 'infrastructure' of a specific language with the ideal 'typological deep structure' (i.e., his metalinguistic standard model) characterizing the particular language type to which that language belongs and within the parametric framework of which it is to be defined.

Instances of implicit or explicit reference to metalinguistic models or parts of such models have been frequent in different contexts and at various stages of linguistic research. Thus, as Uspenskij points out, any statement about the presence of a certain phenomenon in a particular language implies, by itself, an indirect reference to some other language or other languages having the same phenomenon or, at any rate, a ('covert') category of which the given phenomenon is an overt (i.e., surface structure) exponent.[47]

According to Uspenskij one has, further, to distinguish between two types of abstract metalinguistic models of the kind discussed here, a MINIMUM and a MAXIMUM type, respectively. An 'étalon language' of the minimum type is a model which, roughly speaking, amounts to the logical-algebraic (Boolean) PRODUCT of shared structural properties of the languages typologically compared; it can therefore be defined as the overall underlying invariant (constant)

---

[47] In fact, much of our and earlier periods' school grammars are couched in metalinguistic terms. Cf. further B.A. Uspenskij, *Strukturnaja tipologija jazykov*, 60-61 and 241 (with fnn.).

of all these languages (at one or several levels).[48] An 'étalon language' of the maximum type, on the other hand, can be defined as the Boolean SUM of all specific structural features of the languages involved. As a rule, it is the minimum type of abstract metalanguage that will prove to be the most powerful measure of comparison in linguistic typology.

In summary, then, a structural typology of languages is proposed to be set up by matching the generalized structure of a specially devised abstract metalinguistic model (of the minimum or, occasionally, maximum type) with the transformationally established 'infrastructures' of the respective, typologically defined natural languages under scrutiny.[49]

The preceding brief account of some basic principles of a new structural typology of languages, as suggested by Hjelmslev and, along similar lines, further developed by Uspenskij and others, was given here both in view of the general theoretical significance that this new approach merits, and also because its application has already begun to yield some promising concrete results. Thus, in a monograph on the substantive in the Balkan languages, published approximately at the same time as Uspenskij's theoretical study, the concept of an abstract, if partial, metalinguistic model devised to account for a set of shared structural features of several of the

[48] On linguistic invariants and their role in language typology, see further in particular the remarks (commenting on R. Jakobson's Oslo congress paper) by V. V. Ivanov, in: *Proceedings of the Eighth International Congress of Linguists*, 26. Cf. also the 'system-reduction of quantification' of descriptive linguistic comparison, sketched by W. S. Allen, "Relationship in Comparative Linguistics", *Transactions of the Philological Society* (1953), 52-108, esp. 88-100. For some amplification and applications of this approach (*inter alia*, to Balkan linguistics), see J. Ellis, *Towards a General Comparative Linguistics*, esp. 127-133 and 142-153; cf. also E. Levenston and J. O. Ellis, "A Transfer-Grammar Development of System-Reduction Quantified Method", *Zeitschrift für Phonetik, Sprachwissenschaft und Kommunikationsforschung* XVI (1964), 449-452.
[49] See B. A. Uspenskij, *Strukturnaja tipologija jazykov*, 125-143 and, for English summary, 244-246; cf. also the same author's earlier study *Nekotorye voprosy strukturnoj tipologii. Avtoreferat kandidatskoj dissertacii* (Moscow, 1963), esp. 11-12. The notions of minimum and maximum types of metalinguistic models (or 'étalon languages') seem first to have been suggested by A. A. Xolodovič; cf. *Strukturnaja tipologija jazykov*, 63, fn. 1; see further *Voprosy jazykoznanija*, 4 (1965), 74, with reference in fn. 1.

Balkan languages was introduced by T. V. Civ'jan.[50] While this is not the proper place to comment on the apparent merits as well as some shortcomings of the Soviet Balkanologist's work (especially since I have done so elsewhere[51]), it is worth noting, however, that among the most intriguing aspects of her book are precisely the author's remarks pertaining to the possibility of establishing such a fragmentary underlying 'Balkanized' metalinguistic model which would enable us to predict, with some degree of probability, a number of future developments to be expected under 'ideal' conditions in the member languages of the Balkan linguistic convergence area proper, i.e., in Rumanian (including both its Daco-Rumanian bulk and two of its isolated dialects, Arumanian and Megleno-Rumanian), Albanian, Modern Greek as well as Bulgarian and Macedonian, along with the so-called Torlak (or Prizren-Timok) dialect group of Serbo-Croatian.[52] In this context it should be noted, incidentally, that, if we exclude Turkish, the fact that the main Balkan languages are genetically distantly related — all being Indo-European — is almost irrelevant, that is to say, they could virtually be treated as if they were genetically unrelated altogether, since the common 'Balkanisms' all can be assumed to have developed only in the area as evidenced by the circumstance that, say, Rumanian and Bulgarian share a good number of features not found elsewhere in the Romance or Slavic languages, respectively, i.e., outside the Balkans. On the other hand, the close

---

[50] T. V. Civ'jan, *Imja suščestvitel'noe v balkanskix jazykax. K strukturno-tipologičeskoj xarakteristike balkanskogo jazykovogo sojuza* (Moscow, 1965). A preliminary study by the same author, "Opyt opisanija form novogrečeskogo suščestvitel'nogo metodom analiza i sinteza", appeared in *Voprosy jazykoznanija* 6 (1963), 57-68.

[51] See *Zeitschrift für Balkanologie* IV (1966), 173-181; cf. further *Zbornik za filologiju i lingvistiku* IX (1966), 22-24.

[52] Cf. *op. cit.*, 158-191, esp. 183-189; see also my short comments in *International Journal of Slavic Linguistics and Poetics* XI (1968), 21. Cf. in this context further H. Becker's keen, if oversimplified, observation: "Auf dem Balkan haben sich die Sprachen so innig aneinander angepasst, dass die Hauptsprachen der Halbinsel geradezu Wort für Wort ineinander umgesetzt werden können" (*Der Sprachbund* [Berlin–Leipzig, 1948], 24). See now further also V. Blanár, "Über strukturelle Übereinstimmungen im Wortschatz der Balkansprachen", *Recueil linguistique de Bratislava* II (Bratislava, 1968), 80-97.

genetic relationship between Bulgarian, Macedonian, and the 'Balkanized' portion of Serbo-Croatian, notably the Torlak dialects, is no doubt responsible for a number of additional agreements between these Balkan Slavic languages over and above those shared by the South Slavic languages as a whole or, for that matter, by the other Balkan languages or at least some of them.[53]

It must further be stated that if we can agree with Joseph Greenberg and Roman Jakobson that linguistic typology adds to our predictive power[54] and if, moreover, we accept that this assumption can be corroborated by establishing various metalinguistic models (or fragments thereof) devised as a tool in typological linguistics, as suggested by Uspenskij, and that such an abstract model can even be said to underlie or, perhaps rather, to direct the convergent development toward unification and grammatical integration (yielding, in the case of the Balkan languages, an increasingly analytic language structure, as shown for the substantive by Civ'jan), we must at the same time qualify these assumptions by subscribing to the view expressed by one of the critics of Uspenskij who rightly claims that all such typological considerations remain largely theoretical (not to say, academic) as long as the spontaneous development of languages will continue to be determined in large measure by — at least for the linguist — unpredictable forces and factors, frequently amounting to a politically motivated interference of man.[55] Applied to the Balkan linguistic (and political!) situation,

---

[53]   On the 'Balkanization' of Serbo-Croatian and the controversial position of the Torlak dialects, see my remarks in *Zeitschrift für Balkanologie* III (1965), 39-57 ("Das Randgebiet der Balkanismen im südslavischen Sprachraum: das Serbokroatische"), and in *Zbornik za filologiju i lingvistiku* IX (1966), 25-30.

[54]   Cf. J.H. Greenberg, "The Nature and Uses of Linguistic Typologies", *International Journal of American Linguistics* XXIII (1957), 68-77, esp. 77, mentioning also the phenomena of 'drift'; R. Jakobson, *Proceedings of the Eighth International Congress of Linguists*, 23 (= *Selected Writings* I, 528).

[55]   See Ju.V. Roždestvenskij, *Voprosy jazykoznanija* 3 (1966), 115 (in a review of Uspenskij's book); cf. further, for example, also S. Klein, *Mechanical Translation* 9 (1966), 71-72 (the section "Prediction of Historical Events" in his article "Historical Change in Language Using Monte Carlo Techniques"). Generally on linguistic prediction (viewed, with some qualifications, as a correlate of reconstruction, particularly internal reconstruction), see the expanded version of my Bucharest congress paper of 1967, "On Reconstruction

it must thus be said that, while under 'ideal', i.e., undisturbed, conditions one might venture far-reaching predictions as to the future course of development of the languages in this area, the very unpredictability of forthcoming extra-linguistic events that may affect that same area upsets the linguistically inherent probability of any such prophecies, rendering them, in fact, inconclusive.

It was suggested above that an abstract metalinguistic model, usually of the 'minimum' (= Boolean 'product') kind, as sketched by Uspenskij, could serve as the 'typological deep structure' standard against which deviations, at the 'infrastructure' level, of individual member languages of a given, typologically defined language group (such as, for example, the Balkan languages) be measured. This is not to say, however, that such a typological metalinguistic model should be in the form of an inventory of the deep-seated structural properties characteristic of, say, ALL the Balkan languages, thus constituting a closed system. Rather, such a model should be conceived of as an OPEN system and, even more important, not simply as an open-ended LIST of deep-structural 'Balkanisms' but as an expandable SET OF (TRANSFORMATIONAL) RULES by which 'non-Balkan'-type constructions and phrases can be converted into their 'Balkan'-type equivalents. A method for constructing a partial generative grammar of the Balkan languages (as referring to correspondences to some typical uses of the 'European' infinitive) has been proposed by K. Kazazis who has used four non-Balkan languages (English, French, Italian, and Swedish) as 'European' control languages to establish 'Balkan' constructions in Tosk Albanian, Bulgarian, Greek, and Rumanian, the criterion being that "for a given Balkan construction to be included in the grammar, it must be translatable by an infinitival phrase in at least two of the European languages just mentioned."[56] Several impor-

---

and Prediction: Two Correlates of Diachrony in Genetic and Typological Linguistics", *Folia Linguistica* II (1969), 1-17, reprinted below, pp. 71-91; for some general considerations, along similar lines, cf. also E. Pulgram's paper "Trends and Predictions", in: *To Honor Roman Jakobson* II (The Hague, 1967), 1634-1649.

[56] See K. Kazazis, "On a Generative Grammar of the Balkan Languages", *Foundations of Language* 3 (1967), 117-123; this paper is based on its author's

tant advantages of adopting such a method (even with due reservations against some aspects of the control criteria used by Kazazis) are immediately obvious. In particular, as Kazazis has pointed out, many of the most typical 'Balkanisms' seem to be clustered, i.e., occur in relatively small groups of two or three languages whereas the all-embracing 'Balkanisms' (say, the substitution of an original infinitive by a subordinate clause or the use of the originally volitive auxiliary to form the periphrastic future), including also standard Serbo-Croatian at least in its eastern (Serbian) variety, are relatively few.[57] These limited clustered 'Balkanisms' more often than not are found in languages spoken on contiguous territories; the many grammatical (as well as lexical) similarities between Albanian and Daco-Rumanian, however possibly due, in part at least, to earlier geographical vicinity, provide, as is well known, the most conspicuous counter-example. Since the 'Balkanisms' encountered in only two or three languages have a complex and shifting areal distribution (such as 'feature a' is found in languages L_1 and L_2, 'feature b' in L_2 and L_3, 'feature c' in L_1, L_3, and L_4, etc.; cf. also Kazazis' rule count), it is necessary in order to cover all major 'Balkanisms' to devise a generative model in which certain transformations (which can be marked BALKAN 1,

---

unpublished dissertation, *Some Balkan Constructions Corresponding to Western European Infinitives* (Indiana University, 1965).

[57] For these two general Balkan features, cf., for example, K. Sandfeld, *Linguistique balkanique: Problèmes et résultats* (Paris, 1930), 173-185 (they are listed and discussed, of course, in most surveys of 'Balkanisms'). As regards the situation in standard and dialectal Serbo-Croatian, see in particular H. Birn-baum, *Zeitschrift für Balkanologie* III (1965), 53-57. Notice, however, that in several Balkan languages, notably in Albanian and Rumanian (including its Moldavian variety), secondary infinitives have appeared or are about to appear; on this process, cf. especially the important work by M. A. Gabinskij; see, in particular, his monograph *Vozniknovenie infinitiva kak vtoričnyj balkanskij jazykovoj process: Na materiale albanskogo jazyka* (Leningrad, 1967) (with many further references, *inter alia*, to relevant studies by the same author, *ibid.*, 259-260). On some phenomena of secondary "Debalkanization" in contemporary standard Bulgarian (partly under the impact of Russian), see, for example, H. Orzechowska, "Zjawiska wtórnej archaizacji w bułgarskim języku literackim (Z historii zanikania podwójnych dopełnień)", *Z polskich studiów slawistycznych*, Seria 3, *Językoznawstwo* (Warsaw, 1968), 139-151 (with further references).

BALKAN 2, etc., following Kazazis[58]) be added or deleted, which-
ever the case may be for the individual language or languages
discussed. Such a metalinguistic model can thus provide both a
typological and contrastive generative framework. In other words,
once we assume that deep-seated structural properties ('covert
categories') can be assigned to the 'infrastructure' and 'typological
deep structure' levels, respectively (in addition to, in some instances,
being ascertainable in universal 'profound structure') and that 'typological deep structure', therefore, can provide a powerful tool in linguistic typology, as has been proposed in this paper, the necessity or
even need of distinguishing between a strictly 'typological' and a
'contrastive generative' approach to problems of Balkan linguistics,
emphasized by Kazazis,[59] disappears. 'Typological' (suggesting a
somehow unified language type on the basis of similarities and
agreements between individual languages) and 'contrastive' (suggesting a setting apart of languages on the basis of their differences)
must no longer be viewed as mutually exclusive, but rather as
overlapping or, even better, integrated aspects of an overall approach to a specific language group (e.g., the Balkan languages)
and its place within a broader typological classification. Further,
with deep structure (regardless of layer) being conceived of as part
of the semantic component, the distinction between a syntactic and
a specifically semantic component of Balkan generative grammar,
likewise mentioned by Kazazis,[60] becomes largely immaterial or,
rather, confined to the combined operation and interaction of the
(expanded) semantic component and its 'recipient', the transformational (reduced from formerly syntactic) component. The phonological ('symbolization') component of a generative grammar of
the Balkan languages, on the other hand, while embracing at most
a few, if any, pan-Balkan phenomena (including possibly some
prosodic and sentence-intonational features manifested, among

---

[58]   Illustratively applied to a set of rules generating the Balkan constructions
which correspond to the 'without + infinitival phrase' constructions in other
European languages (in English, to 'without + gerund').
[59]   "On a Generative Grammar", 117-118.
[60]   "On a Generative Grammar", 122.

other things, in the typical Balkan proclitics and enclitics[61]), would have to account for a number of instances of convergent distinctive feature treatment (including both assimilation and neutralization as well as some other abstract markedness phenomena) and ought, therefore, to be formulated separately in terms of some common phonological rules applicable to the Balkan linguistic type as a whole.[62] No doubt, an elaborate generative grammar of the Balkan languages, particularly if taking into account also dialectal variations, frequently cutting across standard language boundaries, could by optionally adding further BALKAN-transformations reflect the many characteristic complexities of the Balkan linguistic type far more adequately and in much greater detail than what any traditional ('taxonomic') description of similarities and discrepancies between the in most, but not all, respects convergent languages of this area could reasonably hope to achieve.[63]

As follows even from the preceding few remarks, it appears that by adopting the typological deep structure concept and applying metalinguistic modeling based on this concept to the Balkan linguistic convergence area, new significant insights will be gained into the very nature of the language development in this area, its extent, pace, and direction.

CONCLUDING REMARKS

In conclusion, then, the foregoing discussion can be summed up in the following points:

[61]   Cf. G. Reichenkron, *Zeitschrift für Balkanologie* I (1962), 99-101 (the section "Der Redetaktrhythmus der Balkansprachen" in his article "Der Typus der Balkansprachen"); see further also H.L. Klagstad, "Toward a Morpho-Syntactic Treatment of the Balkan Linguistic Group", *American Contributions to the Fifth International Congress of Slavists*, Vol. I: *Linguistic Contributions* (The Hague, 1963), 179-189. On the pronominal clitics of Balkan Slavic in particular, see now also G.A. Cyxun, *Sintaksis mestoimennyx klitik v južnoslavjanskix jazykax* (*Balkanoslavjanskaja model'*), (Minsk, 1968).
[62]   Cf. K. Kazazis, "On a Generative Grammar", 122; see further also the above quoted dissertation by Afendras (see n. 34).
[63]   The article by J. Schröpfer, "Zur inneren Sprachform der Balkanvölker", *Zeitschrift für Slawistik* I: 4 (1956), 139-151, does not, in spite of its allusion to the Humboldtian concept, treat the Balkan linguistic phenomena from a deep structure point of view.

(1) Language, viewed as a functioning system, can be conceived as a generative model of linguistic structure consisting of two major components, content (the semantic component) and symbolization or expression (the phonological component), the two being linked together by a set of transformations (the transformational component) correlating the abstract deep structures ('covert categories' and their non-linear configurations) with sequential (syntactic) surface structures which in turn, by the application of a number of (morpho-phonological) rewrite rules, can be represented in phonetic (and, secondarily, graphic) symbols, translatable into articulatory-acoustic signals. Deep structure, being semantically based, is integrated into the — expanded — semantic component and does not form part of any syntactic component (in standard theory assumed to exist as a separate, central component of generative grammar); the formerly syntactic component is here reduced to the transformational component connecting content and symbolization and, more specifically, deep structure and (syntactic) surface structure.

(2) Deep structure, heretofore considered largely as being language-universal, must be thought of as multilayered, i.e., consisting of several strata. (a) The most shallow of these deep-structural strata (here tentatively called 'infrastructure') underlies the surface structure of one particular language (as manifested by syntactic synonymy in the surface structure of that language) and is thus language-specific, relatively least generalized (though markedly generalized, of course, as compared to any of the syntactic surface structures expressing it), and relatively most complex or diverse ('rich', viz., in comparison to other layers of deep structure). (b) By contrast, the very deepest stratum (here tentatively called 'profound structure') is truly language-universal and as such differentiating all (natural) language from other semiotic and communicative (i.e., message-transmitting) systems. It is maximally generalized (without, however, becoming amorphous) and relatively least complex or diverse (most 'depleted').[64] (c) Between these two ex-

---

[64] It should perhaps be noted here that there is a qualitative difference between 'universal' and 'general'. Thus even 'maximally generalized' and 'universal'

treme strata of deep structure we can postulate a varying number of intermediate 'typological deep structure' layers corresponding to the shifting number of language types into which individual languages can be globally grouped. Among various typological language groupings, the genetically related languages ('language families', such as the Indo-European) differ, viewed synchronically, from other language groups (among them, those found in linguistic convergence areas, also referred to as *Sprachbünde*, e.g., in the Balkans) primarily insofar as they, in addition to deep-seated, semantically based correlations ('covert category function'), also display a number of superficial, phonologically manifested correspondences, including phonetic sameness ('expression element function'), which only occasionally and to a rather insignificant extent can be found to exist between genetically unrelated languages.

While the integration of deep structure as a whole into the expanded semantic component renders immaterial any attempts at semantic interpretation based on properties or cues found in surface structure (as was recently suggested by Chomsky, cf. Postscript), the proposed stratificational view of deep structure seems to eliminate or at least substantially reduce the problem of alleged loss at the

cannot be considered merely quantitative synonyms. 'Language-universal' is a criterion for defining (natural) language as distinct from other semiotic-communicative systems; 'language-general' (and its derivative, 'generalized'), on the other hand, simply indicates that something is peculiar to many, most, or all languages of the world. 'Profound structure' is thus BOTH 'universal' AND 'maximally generalized' while various 'typological deep structure' strata are merely — more or less — 'generalized'. On the distinction between 'universal' and (more or less) 'general' as related to semantics (and hence to deep structure), cf. Y. Bar-Hillel, "Universal Semantics", 9-10, proposing to use (absolute, maximal) 'generality' to denote 'accidental allness', 'universality' to denote 'necessary allness'. In Bar-Hillel's words, "a given linguistic feature would be termed universal, rather than just general, not simply because the state of affairs was such and not otherwise, but rather because we would not want to call something a language unless it contained that feature, in other words, if the occurrence of that feature was necessitated by the very meaning of the term 'language'." For some critical thoughts on language universals and universal grammar, as conceived, on the one hand, by J. Greenberg and, on the other, by the transformational-generative school, see now also A. Martinet, "Réflexions sur les universaux du langage", *Folia Linguistica* I (1967 [1969]), 125-134, further developing some ideas contained already in Hjelmslev's *Prolegomena*.

(uniform) deep structure level of features or categories represented in the surface structure (a claim which, among other things, has led some generative grammarians of the younger generation to question the validity of positing deep structure altogether). Thus, some of these features and categories, while, to be sure, irretrievable or, rather, indiscernible in the universal 'profound structure', can be ascertained in 'typological deep structure' (of varying 'depth' and generality) or in shallow 'infrastructure'. The virtual identification up to now of all (i.e., undifferentiated) deep structure with universal (i.e., in the terminology adopted here, 'profound') deep structure seems to stem largely from insufficient elaboration of deep structures of languages other than Indo-European (the latter representing a comprehensive and widely ramified language type among the languages of the world).

(3) The correlations found at one or another 'typological deep structure' level of two or more languages (and thus defining these languages as being members of a given linguistic type) are shown to coincide largely with what Hjelsmlev termed 'category function', the basic criterion advanced by him for establishing typological relationship between languages (as opposed to '[expression] element function' to ascertain genetic relationship). Adopting a felicitous coinage by Fillmore, the term 'covert category' to denote a category of deep structure is introduced. Different kinds and ranges of linguistic types, including those characterized by genetic relationship (and thus allowing for typologies also of genetically related languages, e.g., the Slavic) are discussed and shown partly to coincide and/or overlap (cf. relationships such as those obtaining between Indo-European, Slavic, South Slavic, Balkan, with the latter including, again, essentially Indo-European languages only). A typological deep structure approach also to genetically related languages (such as the Indo-European) is claimed to yield new important insights also into the reconstruction of protolinguistic (here, Proto-Indo-European) syntax. This is demonstrated on the so-called absolute case constructions (equivalent syntactically to a subordinate clause) of early and archaic Indo-European (Ancient Greek, Latin, Old Church Slavic, medieval and dialectal East

Slavic, Lithuanian, Gothic, etc.) where — as noticed also by Andersen — a common Indo-European (typological) deep structure can be assumed to have existed manifesting itself in semantically and morphologically conditioned different choices of case (genitive, ablative, dative). Reference is further made to recent work showing deep structure agreements among such languages as Latin, Romance, notably Spanish, and English.

(4) The notions of 'typological deep structure' and '(covert) category function' can be considered cornerstones in a new approach to linguistic typology, that of metalinguistic modeling. Using an abstract metalinguistic model as a standard for measuring the cohesiveness (or distance) of typologically related (= structurally isomorphic) languages, as was suggested by Uspenskij, new insights can be gained into the nature and evolutionary trend of such language groups. In particular, this approach can be applied to linguistic convergence areas, as that found in the Balkans. A method, similar to that proposed by Uspenskij, has thus been successfully used by Civ'jan to describe the grammatical integration of the substantive in the Balkan languages, its extent and limits. However, to ensure maximum coverage of the complexities and intricacies of all the unevenly distributed 'Balkanisms' determining the varied Balkan linguistic convergence area, metalinguistic modeling should be in terms of an open set of (transformational) rules, roughly along lines suggested by Kazazis, rather than in the form of a closed inventory of Balkan features.

Finally, one more note on the relationship of genetic and typological linguistics. My earlier contention that there can be only two valid general sets of criteria for language classification, namely, genetic and typological — but not also a third one of the same order, viz., areal, since spatial considerations can at most play a subsidiary role in language grouping[65] — could be upheld only if 'typological' were to be understood in a narrow sense of something like 'structurally kindred due to reasons other than genetic relation-

[65]   Cf. H. Birnbaum, *Zeitschrift für Balkanologie* III (1965), 60; *Zbornik za filologiju i lingvistiku* IX (1966), 17-18.

ship'. However, if we are to adopt 'typological' (relationship, grouping, etc.) as a global concept, following suggestions made in this paper, such a narrow interpretation becomes misleading and, consequently, inadequate. Rather, 'genetic relationship' of languages should be viewed as one — and, to be sure, a very specific one — among several conceivable forms of 'typological relationship', thus allowing for the positing also of such language TYPES as the Indo-European, the Slavic, etc.[66] Perhaps, in realizing the hierarchical superiority of linguistic typology over genetic (or 'historical-comparative') linguistics, the time has now come to slightly rephrase the once relevant question "What can typological studies contribute to historical comparative linguistics?", answered by Roman Jakobson with great insight and eloquence before the world community of linguists over a decade ago,[67] to read: what can genetic linguistics, as an integral part of typological linguistics, contribute to a fuller and better understanding of language typology as a whole? For, in the last analysis, a global typological linguistics is, as Louis Hjelmslev so clearly foresaw it, the only basis upon which universal linguistics and, consequently, a valid general theory of language can rest.[68]

POSTSCRIPT

In a recent, as yet unpublished paper (circulated privately and brought to my attention only after the bulk of the present study

[66]   J. Greenberg, in his recent contribution "Some Methods of Dynamic Comparison in Linguistics", *Substance and Structure of Language*, 147-203, while concerned primarily with surface and symbolization (phonological) phenomena, also suggests a 'dynamic' or 'processual' comparativism in typological confrontations which goes beyond the genetic/typological cleavage, proposing instead a unified, global approach.

[67]   Cf. R. Jakobson, "Typological Studies and Their Contribution to Historical Comparative Linguistics", in: *Proceedings of the Eighth International Congress of Linguists*, 17-35 (including discussion); reprinted in his *Selected Writings* I, 523-531. For an assessment of some of the most crucial implications of Jakobson's report, see also the contribution to the discussion by V. V. Ivanov (*op. cit.*, 25-27); cf. also my remarks in *Scando-Slavica* XIII (1967), 114; and, similarly, in *International Journal of Slavic Linguistics and Poetics* XI (1968), 21-22; *Glossa* 2:1 (1968); 87-88; and *Folia Linguistica* II (1969), 1 (reprinted below, p. 71).

[68]   Cf. the quotation opening the present paper.

was written; to appear in the *Festschrift for S. Hattori*), "Deep Structure, Surface Structure, and Semantic Interpretation", N. Chomsky has provided a fairly elaborate defense against recent attacks on deep structure as this concept was formulated in what he now refers to as the 'standard theory'. Since it was too late for me to incorporate my critique of Chomsky's important, though rather inconclusive recent contribution in the main body of the text of the present paper, the reader is asked for his indulgence with the following comment in the form of a postscript. Chomsky's argumentation is directed, in particular, against the objections raised by McCawley (based largely on an alleged equivocation in the use of the 'respectively-transformation') and by Lakoff (using the claimed non-deep-seatedness of instrumental adverbs to illustrate that deep structure will contain many fewer grammatical categories and relations than had been previously believed and that, thus depleted, deep structure would be much more abstract, i.e., farther removed from surface structure, than had been originally thought). In general, Chomsky's counter-arguments seem, at least to me, reasonably cogent. But some further elaborations of his theory deserve mention, especially, his initial definition of "a grammar of a language... as a system of rules that expresses the correspondence between SOUND AND MEANING [emphasis added] in this language" and, moreover, his definition of a lexicon as "a class of lexical entries each of which specifies the grammatical (i.e., phonological, semantic and syntactic) properties of some lexical item", with "each lexical entry" thought of "as incorporating a set of transformations that insert the item in question (that is, the complex of features that constitutes it) in phrase-markers". Chomsky distinguishes now, in other words, between lexical and nonlexical (i.e., grammatical or truly syntactic) transformations. Applied to the model of linguistic structure outlined above, this would mean that we must assume two transformational components: one lexical-transformational subcomponent operating within the larger semantic component and generating 'postlexical' (i.e., deep) structure; and another, syntactic-transformational component converting deep ('postlexical') into surface structure and thus linking content with expression, meaning with sound. While not without some significant repercussions, this development of transformational-generative theory seems, on the whole, acceptable.

However, in Chomsky's recent elaboration and modification of his 'standard theory' there are also some important points where I cannot fully agree with him. Thus, in discussing the recent suggestions favoring a 'semantically based' theory of generative grammar over a 'syntactically based' one Chomsky plays down to nil the significance of any order or direction of sentence generation or structure and representation mapping in a competence model of language. We are told that "the standard theory generates quadruples (P, s, d, S) (P a phonetic representation, s a surface structure, d a deep structure, S a semantic representation). It is meaningless to ask whether it does so by 'first' generating d, then mapping it onto S (on one side) and onto s and then P (on the other); or whether it 'first' generates S (selecting it, however one wishes, from the universal set of semantic representations), and then maps it onto d, then s, then P; or, for that matter, whether it 'first 'selects the pair (P, d) which is then mapped onto the pair (s, S), etc. ... There is no general notion 'direction of mapping' or 'order of steps of generation' to which one can appeal in attempting to differentiate the 'syntactically based' standard theory from the 'semantically based' alternative, or either from the 'alternative view' which regards the pairing of surface structure and semantic interpretation as determined by the 'independently selected' pairing of phonetic representation and deep structure, etc." Even if limited to a competence model of language, such virtually complete arbitrariness as to the point of departure for any sentence generation or description of structure and representation mapping would thus render insubstantial the existing, and I believe essential, difference, pointed out above, between the order or direction of generative processes (and rules formalizing them) in Chomskyan 'standard theory' and Chafe's model of linguistic structure. Consequently, the selection of a 'reading' (i.e., semantic representation) of a given sentence could serve as the 'first' step in a complex generative process or formal characterization equally well as could an 'initial' generation of deep structure or even a 'first' selection of matching phonetic representation and deep structure to be mapped onto the matching surface structure and semantic representation ('reading'), etc. This, as it were, total cancellation of direction (in a competence model of language) seems to cast some serious doubt upon the whole concept of language as a 'creative' faculty of man (approximating Humboldt's *energeia*), expressible and formalizable in terms of various sets of generative rules, rather than merely a structure assumed to exist so to speak independently, i.e., as something given beforehand (comparable to Humboldt's *ergon*). Many of us have presumably taken for granted the obvious merits of a generative approach to linguistic structure, without, however, necessarily interpreting it as implying a contrast between two mutually exclusive aspects of language (viz., the generative vs. the 'taxonomic') but merely viewing it as supplementing one major aspect of linguistic structure (viz., analysis, classification and segmentation) with another at least equally important one (synthesis, 'process', in the post-Bloomfieldian rather than Hjelmslevian sense of the term). The modified, choiceless and orderless interpretation of sentence generation would, however, seem to invalidate this whole approach. Chomsky, who better than anyone else has succeeded in demonstrating the insight- and powerfulness of the generative view of language, will have to accept the fact that many of his followers will find it increasingly difficult to accompany him on what appears to be the road to destruction of the very foundations of his own theory.

A good portion of Chomsky's paper, roughly its second half, is devoted to an apparently important modification of the 'standard theory', largely following from the alleged arbitrariness as to priority of components in the interrelated generative processes. As I remain unconvinced of this arbitrariness, I also fail to see the significance of Chomsky's suggested further modification of his theory. I am referring to the discussion of instances where, according to him, semantic interpretation seems to hinge more directly on surface structure than on deep structure. The instances discussed (and exemplified) include cases of 'focus' vs. 'presupposition' (marked by stress and sentence intonation and involving such phenomena as contrastive and/or expressive intonation); the scope of logical elements, primarily negation and certain quantifiers (claimed to be largely determined by their position in surface structure); modal (or, rather, modal-temporal) auxiliaries, particularly when combined with negation; anaphoric and other reference processes (again, with surface structure stress and position rather than any deep structure properties said to play a determining role); the 'perfect aspect' (obviously meant either as the perfect tense or, possibly, as the perfective aspect implicit in the perfect), where the semantic interpretation, once more, is claimed to be susceptible to disambiguation only by recourse to certain surface properties, especially if coordination is involved as well; change of forms of the verb *to be*, particularly if combined with insertion or position alteration of the word *even*. According to Chomsky, if we reject the Saussurian view that a sentence is constructed by a series of successive choices, "there is no reason at all why properties of surface structure should not play a role in determining semantic interpretation", so much more if we also take into account the "filtering function" of transformations and posit transformations mapping "base structures into well-formed structures close to surface structures meeting the requirement of a phrase structure grammar".

This is not the place to examine all the cases adduced by Chomsky causing him to modify his earlier model of the deep structure — semantic interpretation — semantic representation ('reading') correlation by admitting properties of surface structure (or, more generally, information not represented in deep structure) as partly determining interpretation. Needless to say, all these problems are demonstrated and illustrated entirely on English linguistic data. Let me only say that, as far as I can see, the "surface structure properties" claimed by Chomsky to contribute to determine semantic interpretation do not, in fact, need to be considered as such. Rather, they all represent surface expressions (at the syntactic surface level or partly even closer to the symbolization surface proper, i.e., in the phonetic representation, e.g., in the case of stress and intonational sentence contour) of some underlying, as yet poorly-understood deep structure properties. However, the very difficulty of identifying, isolating, and formalizing certain deep-seated features, complexes, or relations does not, by itself, suggest that they do not exist in the deep structure. Quite the contrary, we would be unwise not to admit that our knowledge of deep structure is still, in many respects, very vague and largely intuitive. For example, several of the phenomena enumerated by Chomsky seem to fall within the domain of what sometimes has been labeled 'functional sentence perspective', i.e., the theme/rheme or topic/comment organization of sentences, drawing on information (and expectancy) contained in a broader context of the discourse (i.e., set of utterances). Despite some quite significant progress in this field of linguistic research, both by members of the Prague School — earlier especially V. Mathesius, in more recent years J. Firbas and others — and the London School — foreshadowed, in a way, by J. R. Firth's 'structural order' of expectancy, not always closely matching temporal sequence (and thus related also to Chomskyan deep structure), more recently in particular M. A. K. Halliday — much of the information-theoretical and 'suprasyntactic' sentence organization still escapes rigorous formalization and partly even resists unambiguous interpretation. This does not mean, however, that factors of suprasentential information structure must not be taken into consideration. While Chomsky, to be sure, makes some vague reference also to "such matters as ... topic and comment" (see esp. his note 32), this whole framework is not utilized in any systematic manner in the discussion of the allegedly surface structure-related instances of semantic interpretation. Yet it seems that 'functional sentence perspective' (or the information-bearing structure of the sentence in its broader discourse context), while manifested in surface structure by means such as word order, emphatic stress, etc., must be assumed to be represented in deep structure; and the fact that these deep-seated properties and relations still need to be exhibited and mapped out in a detailed and systematic manner does not, of course, constitute an argument against such a supposition. Thus, Chomsky's own 'focus'/'presupposition' distinction is clearly related to the topic/comment (or theme/rheme) opposition implicit in 'functional sentence perspective', as, incidentally, also corroborated by Chomsky's own statement that "choice of focus determines the relation of the utterance to responses, to utterances to which it is a possible response, and to other sentences in the discourse." Of most recent contributions to the topic/comment problem viewed in a generative framework, see Ö. Dahl, *Topic and Comment: A Study in Russian and General Transformational Grammar* (Gothenburg, 1969). It is far from sure, however, that Chomsky sees the cause-effect relation underlying the choice of focus in the way suggested (if he sees any such relation here at all). Likewise, I fail to see that "the scope of negation will be determined by the position of 'not' in surface structure." While the observation that 'negation of (a whole) proposition' and 'negation of the VP' (i.e., of the predicate) do not always coincide is no doubt both important and correct, the place of the negation in surface structure is, in my opinion, not primary but merely a — secondary — expression (or function) of the underlying deep structure, and, ultimately, of the meaning or 'message' to be conveyed. Furthermore, the fact that in languages where the discrimination between a modal and a temporal use of auxiliaries may be tenuous, as is the case in English (*shall, will*), the addition of an element of negation often implies a 'modalization' of the given expression (cf. Chomsky's examples (88i, 88ii) *John will go downtown* vs. *John won't go downtown*) is quite well known also from other languages at different stages of their development (a comparable phenomenon in Old Church Slavic and, correspondingly, in postclassical Greek was discussed at some length in my *Untersuchungen zu den Zukunftsumschreibungen mit dem Infinitiv im Altkirchenslavischen* [Stockholm, 1958], 217-220). While it is true that Chomsky's example (89) *John can't seem to get his homework done on time* lacks a formal positive (non-negated) counterpart, this is due, of course, to the defective nature of *can* (lacking an infinitive form) in English surface structure, which explains its anomalous place and function in the quoted sentence. Clearly, the suggested paraphrases (90) *it seems that John can't get his homework done on time* / *that John is unable to get his homework done on time,* which allow for positive counterparts, indicate that the anomalous surface structure of (89) has a deep structure from which the negation can be extracted. The anaphoric and other reference processes exemplified by Chomsky can, as in previous instances, be interpreted in terms of an underlying information-theoretical structure going beyond the boundaries of one single sentence. The claimed surface structure-related semantic interpretation of sentences with the 'perfect aspect' seem little convincing as Chomsky's 'has died'-test is open to different 'readings'. Finally, it is anything but clear why the change in tense and/or mood of the copula — say, *is* to *would be* in a sentence such as (112) *John is* ⇒ *would be tall for a Watusi* — or the insertion or position shift of 'even', undoubtedly altering the semantic interpretation of the sentence, are not relatable to corresponding (and, in my view, primary) modifications in the deep structure. Thus, for example, the *is* ⇒ *would be* transformation implies the addition of (a marked) modality (or the replacement of one modality by another, say, unmarked 'indicativeness' or 'objectivity' by marked 'unreality' or something of that sort) in the underlying deep structure. Nothing suggests, it would seem, that these changes take place merely or, rather, 'first' in the surface structure.

The lengthy excursus contained in this Postscript should suffice, it is hoped, to indicate why in the main text of this paper, while recognizing our fragmentary knowledge of the nature of deep structure, I would continue to assign to it roughly the status it has in 'standard theory' of Chomskyan generative grammar rather than, with McCawley and Lakoff, question the very justification for positing it or, following Chomsky's recent reasoning, impair its exclusive function of mapping semantically interpreted 'readings' onto (syntactic) surface structure. What is different in my view of deep structure as compared to the 'standard theory' is essentially that I, along with some other semantically oriented linguists, conceive of deep structure as forming a part (subcomponent) of an enlarged semantic component in which it holds an intermediate position between an abstract and only latent semantic representation ('reading') and what in Chomskyan terminology is referred to as the base subcomponent or system, in turn subdivided into the lexical and categorial subsystems, both providing deep structure with the 'material' of which it is made up. Deep structure generates (as input to the transformational or, if we are to assume also lexical transformational processes at work, the syntactic or nonlexical transformational component) structures converted into initial (or syntactic) surface structures (as output of the transformational component) to be then further refined in symbolization and eventually assume phonetic (or other perceptible, e.g., graphic) shape in the ('rewrite') processes of going through the various levels of the phonological component (graphic representation of phonetic representation implying an extension of the phonological component by one or several further levels of representation, depending on how 'phonetic' a given writing system is).

The stratificational view of deep structure as elaborated in this paper (and believed to yield an important tool for linguistic typology) is suggested to add a new dimension to the deep structure concept (essentially modifying, among other things, its implicit if not explicit claim to universality) but does not otherwise fundamentally change the overall scope or function of this subcomponent of generative grammar as such.

ON RECONSTRUCTION AND PREDICTION:
TWO CORRELATES OF DIACHRONY IN GENETIC
AND TYPOLOGICAL LINGUISTICS

1. Over ten years ago, at the Eighth International Congress of Linguists, Roman Jakobson in the concluding section of his memorable report on "Typological Studies and Their Contribution to Historical Comparative Linguistics" quoted Joseph Greenberg's view that linguistic typology adds to "our predictive power since from a given synchronic system certain developments will be highly likely, other have less probability and still others may be practically excluded". Moreover, Jakobson in this context reminded his audience of the image conceiving of the historian as a prophet predicting backward, a paradox framed some century and a half ago by Friedrich Schlegel, one of the great heralds of genetic as well as typological linguistics.[1]

Since Jakobson made these references much work has been done both in the study of linguistic genealogy and typology. New theoretical insights have been reached and hitherto untested methods have been applied in both fields. Thus, among other things, the realization that synchrony does not, in fact, preclude certain dynamics inherent in linguistic structure (or in some sub-structure of a language system) at a given time has led linguists to refine and deepen their interpretation of linguistic change on the basis of synchronic data. In particular, inferences based on data from a single language at a certain stage of its development have been increasingly utilized for the purpose of recovering unrecorded

[1] Cf. *Proceedings of the Eighth International Congress of Linguists* (Oslo, 1958), 23; reprinted in R. Jakobson, *Selected Writings* I (The Hague, 1962), 528 (section 6: "Typology and Reconstruction").

protolanguages as well as lost phases in the history (or prehistory) of individual languages, accidentally or for well-established extra-linguistic reasons not attested in writing. This method, usually referred to as INTERNAL RECONSTRUCTION, has already yielded considerable results in the field of phonology and morphophono-logy (if the latter may be singled out as a special branch of linguis-tics and not merely be considered a part of phonology [N. Chomsky, M. Halle] or morphology [A. Martinet]) while the applicability of this method to other levels or strata of language has not yet been sufficiently tested. In general, the outcome of internal reconstruc-tion has served to supplement and corroborate such linguistic reconstruction as has been arrived at by more traditional proce-dures, viz., by those of the comparative method. Suffice it to refer in this context to the work on the theory and application of internal reconstruction done over the last decade by scholars such as H. Hoenigswald, W. Lehmann, W. Chafe in America, J. Kuryło-wicz, T. Milewski, V. Ivanov in Europe, to mention just a few.[2] As is generally known, internal reconstruction has been shown to be particularly useful for the establishing of RELATIVE CHRONOLOGY as regards various processes of mutation whereas the very nature of its basic linguistic data, allowing for a projection backward in time only, virtually rules out any possibility of arriving at new results bearing on absolute chronology.

2. In recent years, attempts have been made to demonstrate the non-accidental character of the partial parallelism obtaining be-

[2]   Cf., *i. a.*, H.M. Hoeningswald, *Language Change and Linguistic Recon-struction* (Chicago, 1959), *passim*, esp. 99-104; W.P. Lehmann, *Historical Lin-guistics: an Introduction* (New York, 1962), 99-106; *Id.*, "Vyvody o proto-indoevropejskoj glagol'noj sisteme, osnovannye na vnutrennem analize san-skrita", *Voprosy jazykoznanija* 2, (1961), 24-27; W.L.Chafe, "Internal Re-construction in Seneca", *Language* 35 (1959), 477-495; J. Kuryłowicz, "On the Methods of Internal Reconstruction" (with discussion), *Proceedings of the Ninth International Congress of Linguists* (The Hague, 1964), 9-36; T. Milewski, *Językoznawstwo* (Warsaw, 1965), 138-139; V.V. Ivanov and V.N.Toporov, "K postanovke voprosa o drevnejšix otnošenijax baltijskix i slavjanskix jazykov", *Issledovanija po slavjanskomu jazykoznaniju* (Moscow, 1961), 273-305; V.V. Ivanov, *Obščeindoevropejskaja, praslavjanskaja i anatolijskaja ja-zykovye sistemy (sravnitel'no-tipologičeskie očerki)* (Moscow, 1965), *passim*.

tween relative chronology of sound change (as established primarily by means of internal reconstruction) and the, to some degree, fixed order of phonological rules, as the latter are now being elaborated for various languages within the framework of transformational generative grammar. I am referring here to explicit statements and cursory hints to this effect in the writings of N. Chomsky, M. Halle, T. Lightner, E. Klima, S. Saporta, B. Sigurd, N. E. Enkvist, B. Malmberg, A. Zaliznjak, myself, and others.[3] If indeed shown to

[3] Cf., e.g., N. Chomsky, "Topics in the Theory of Generative Grammar", *Current Trends in Linguistics* III (The Hague–Paris, 1966), 57; M. Halle, "On the Role of Simplicity in Linguistic Descriptions", *Structure of Language and its Mathematical Aspects: Proceedings of the Twelfth Symposium in Applied Mathematics*, R. Jakobson (ed.) (Providence, R. I., 1961), 89-94, esp. 92-94; *Id.*, "Phonology in Generative Grammar", *Word* 18 (1962), 54-72, esp. 66-72 (with slight modifications reprinted in *The Structure of Language: Readings in the Philosophy of Language*, J. A. Fodor and J. J. Katz [eds.] [Englewood Cliffs, N.J., 1964], 334-352, esp. 346-352); *Id.*, "O pravilax russkogo sprjaženija", *American Contributions to the Fifth International Congress of Slavists* I (The Hague, 1963), 113-132, esp. 127; T. M. Lightner, "Preliminary Remarks on the Morphophonemic Component of Polish", *Quarterly Progress Report* (MIT, Research Laboratory of Electronics), 71 (1963), 220-235; *Id.*, "O cikličeskix pravilax v russkom sprjaženii" *Voprosy jazykoznanija* 2, (1965), 45-54, esp. 51-54; *Id.*, "On the Phonology of the Old Church Slavonic Conjugation", *International Journal of Slavic Linguistics and Poetics* X (1966), 1-28, esp. 23-26; *Id.*, "Ob al'ternacii *e* ~ *o* v sovremennom russkom literaturnom jazyke", *Voprosy jazykoznanija* 5, (1966), 64-80; and some further work by the same linguist. An announced joint paper by Halle and Lightner, "Relative Chronology and Synchronic Order of Rules", has not appeared to date; E. S. Klima, "Relatedness between Grammatical Systems", *Language* 40 (1964), 1-20, esp. 2; S. Saporta, "Ordered Rules, Dialect Differences, and Historical Processes", *Language* 41 (1965), 218-224; B. Sigurd, "Generative Grammar and Historical Linguistics", *Acta Linguistica Hafniensia* X (1966), 35-48; N. E. Enkvist, "Tre modeller för ljudhistorisk forskning", *Societas Scientiarum Fennica* XLIV B, 4 (1966); B. Malmberg, 'Synchronie et diachronie', *Actes du Xe Congrès international des linguistes*, I (Bucharest, 1969), 13-36 (including discussion), esp. 17; A. A. Zaliznjak, "O vozmožnoj svjazi meždu operacionnymi ponjatijami sinxronnogo opisanija i diaxroniej", *Simpozium po strukturnomu izučeniju znakovyx sistem* (Moscow, 1962; not available to me for page reference); *Id.*, "Sinxronnoe opisanie i vnutrennjaja rekonstrukcija", *Problemy sravnitel'noj grammatiki indoevropejskix jazykov: Naučnaja sessija: Tezisy dokladov* (Moscow, 1964), 51-54; H. Birnbaum, "Rekonstrukcja wewnętrzna, kolejność synchronicznych reguł gramatyki syntetycznej i zagadnienie najdawniejszych stosunków między językami bałtyckimi a słowiańskimi", *International Journal of Slavic Linguistics and Poetics* XI (1968), 1-24. A revised English version of

be valid, the application of fully or partially ordered phonological rules could, with some necessary qualifications, be considered a METHOD OF PREDICTING instances of subsequent linguistic change. Since the actual outcome is previously known, the reliability of the procedure can easily be checked and inadequacies rectified. This method of arriving at synchronically observable morphophonemic alternations on the basis of underlying forms to which a set of generative phonological rules is applied can thus be viewed as paralleling, if only to some extent, the method of internal reconstruction. However, under no circumstances can we here assume a full parallelism, that is, a complete and consistent recapitulation — by means of a set of ordered rules — of a series of actual historical sound changes as recoverable by internal (as well as comparative) reconstruction. Rather, it seems reasonable to consider a broad parallelism, allowing for occasional deviations but including, on the other hand, instances where an arbitrariness in the order of application of the phonological rules shows a close correlation with the frequent insufficiency of internal criteria for establishing any indisputable relative chronology. Examples of such correlation in terms of arbitrariness with regard to the order of descriptive generative rules (of the phonological component) and relative chronology (of sound change) based on internal reconstruction, respectively, have recently been supplied by, among others, Chafe (for Seneca, a language of the Iroquoian group of American Indian languages), Sigurd (for Old Swedish), and myself (for Common Slavic).[4]

Consider, by way of illustration, some of the forms of the paradigm represented by OCS *otьcь* 'father': Nom. sg. *otьcь*, Gen. sg.

this paper appears now on pp. 92-122 of the present volume. Cf. now also the paper by V. J. Zeps, "A Synchronic and Diachronic Order of Rules: Mutations of Velars in Old Church Slavonic", in *Approaches in Linguistic Methodology*, I. Rauch and Ch. T. Scott (eds.) (Madison, Milwaukee-London, 1967), 145-151, highly skeptical of ANY non-accidental parallelism between synchronic and diachronic order of rules.

[4] Cf. W. L. Chafe, *Explorations in the Theory of Language* (forthcoming; end of section 5. 11. in preliminary draft); for a similar reasoning as applied to Caddo, another American Indian language, see now also *Id.*, *Language* 43 (1967), 67-73. For references to the papers of Sigurd and myself, see fn. 3.

otьc'a (*otьcä*), Instr. sg. *otьcetь*, Loc. sg. *otьci*, Voc. sg. *otьče*;
Nom. pl. *otьci*. Clearly, in the case of the Nom., Gen., Instr.,
Loc. sg. we have instances of the so-called third (progressive)
'Baudouin' palatalization: *otьcь* < **otьkъ*, *otьc'a* < **otьka*,
otьcetь < **otьkomь*, *otьci* < **otьkě* (< **atikoi*, cf. *rabě*, *vlьcě*).
All the above reconstructed forms are suggested by the parallellism
of the regular *o-* and *jo-*stems (*rabъ* : *kon'ь*, etc.). The origin of
the Nom. pl. form, on the other hand, is ambiguous: either it, too,
represents the *jo-*stem type (*kon'i*), or we have to do here with an
instance of the so-called second (regressive) palatalization of velars
in Common Slavic: *otьci* < **atikoi* (cf. *rabi*, *vlьci*), where *k* > *c*
before a secondary front vowel, in this case *-i* < *-oi*. As for the
Voc. sg., it is obviously the result of the so-called first (regressive)
palatalization: *otьče* < **otьke* (or earlier **atike*), with *k* > *č* before a primary (original) front vowel, here *e*. Now, while the chronological relationship of forms like the Nom. (Gen., Instr., Loc.)
sg. (*otьcь*, etc.) and the Voc. sg. (*otьče*) can be accounted for by
applying appropriate generative phonological rules, the chronological ambiguity as regards the origin of the Nom. pl. form (*otьci*)
will not be resolved by the application of any such synchronic
phonological rule. Thus, one could formulate the following rules,
to be applied in this order:

(1) *ke* → *če*,
(2) *ьk* → *ьc*,
(3) *cъ* → *cь*,
  ca → *c'a* (*cä*),
  co → *ce*,
  cě → *ci*.

In fact, these three rules suffice to produce the quoted Old Church
Slavic forms of the *otьcь* paradigm (assuming an underlying stem
*otьk-):

	After application of rule 1	/ of rule 2	/ of rule 3
Nsg. **otьkъ*	→ **otьkъ*	→ **otьcъ*	→ *otьcь*
Gsg. **otьka*	→ **otьka*	→ **otьca*	→ *otьc'a* (*otьcä*)
Isg. **otьkomь*	→ **otьkomь*	→ **otьcomь*	→ *otьcemь*

Lsg. *otъkě (< *atikoi) → *otъkě → *otъcě → otъci
Vsg. *otъke → otъče → otъče → otъče
Npl. *otъki (< *atikoi) → *otъki → otъci → otъci

It will be noticed that the correct (i.e., attested) form of the Voc. sg. is generated already by the application of rule 1, and the correct form of the Nom. pl. by the application of rule 2. However, it is quite possible that the correct Nom. pl. form actually should have resulted from the application of an additional earlier rule, to be inserted between rule 1 and rule 2 (in the above numbering), viz., a rule 1a to the effect that $-ki_2$ (i.e., $-ki < -koi$) → $-ci$, thus complicating the generative process. As relative chronology of the so-called second (regressive) and third (progressive) palatalizations of velars, based on internal criteria, remains controversial (and, rather, external criteria and absolute chronology seem to suggest the usually assumed chronological order of these changes), there is nothing in the order of synchronic phonological rules to in any way determine the order of occurrence of the two later Common Slavic palatalizations.[5]

However, in such cases where regular techniques of internal reconstruction may fail, owing to lack of sufficiently complete data or improper diachronic interpretation of such data, the application of an ordered set of appropriate phonological rules (generating some, if not all, of the observed morphophonemic alternations) can occasionally serve as a powerful heuristic device for establishing at least a tentative chronology of sound change.[6]

One of the main and obvious differences between, on the one hand, formulating phonological rules to account for subsequent morphophonemic alternations and, on the other, establishing, to the extent possible, a relative chronology by means of internal

---

[5] For further details on the problem of Common Slavic phonology discussed here, see my paper "Rekonstrukcja wewnętrzna ..." (cf. fn. 3, above, and pp. 92-122, below).

[6] We can therefore fully subscribe to B. Sigurd's view: "It is probably fair to say that we may base an educated guess as to some historical changes on the rules of a synchronic generative grammar of the language. By the same token knowledge of the history of the language may help in constructing a synchronic generative grammar of a certain stage."; "Generative Grammar", 36; cf. also ibid., 46.

reconstruction is that in the case of setting up predictive (generative) rules the point of departure is provided by some theoretical underlying 'protoforms' (input forms), as yet unaffected by any descriptive rule, with the phonological rules themselves only being formulated on the basis of our *ex post facto* knowledge of the actual resulting synchronic alternations whereas, in the case of internal reconstruction proper, the basic linguistic data are precisely the ascertainable forms yielded by an historical process of linguistic change. Thus, the two approaches' respective orientations on the time axis are contrary ones. The method of generating actually observable forms showing morphophonemic alternations may be subsumed under the more general method of PROJECTIVE PREDICTION, a term which, however, also could be conceived to include a formal interpretation of certain predictable trends of subsequent linguistic evolution based on typological or, more specifically, areal-typological rather than genetic criteria, as will be discussed below.

A further question deserving consideration is whether such projective prediction of linguistic change can be based on synchronic data not only in terms of using as a point of departure hypothetic 'protoforms' admittedly far from always coinciding with such prehistoric forms as arrived at by means of linguistic reconstruction, internal or comparative[7] — but also on the basis of data ascertainable in the present, conceiving of the present as another 'synchronic slice' and projecting, as it were, these data into the future. This, then, would allow us to view internal reconstruction and projective prediction (particularly if shown to be extendible beyond the limits of phonology and morphophonology) as at least partly correlative approaches to diachronic linguistics at large. In other words, both approaches being based on the intrinsic dynamics of synchrony (as conceived in the present), they would differ primarily only in terms of their opposite orientation on the time axis: internal reconstruction pointing backward — into the past, projective prediction forward — into the future. Needless to say, the purpose of formulating such phonological rules on the basis of synchronic data of the

---

[7] Cf., e.g., T.M. Lightner's relevant statements in *International Journal of Slavic Linguistics and Poetics* X (1966), 25, with fn. 41.

present, rather than on the basis of some assumed underlying 'proto-forms', would be an entirely different one and, at any rate, not to account for any morphophonemic alternations in the future. Yet, it seems somewhat doubtful whether the formulation of such strictly theoretical future-oriented generative phonological rules can be accomplished without recourse to verification by means of any readily ascertainable outcome.

3. Before attempting to explore any further implications of this tentative conception, a few words may be said about some recent developments in typological linguistics, that is, in the other main sphere of our discipline commented upon by Jakobson in the report previously referred to. Particularly, I would like to mention two pertinent aspects of general linguistic typology that have been brought into the fore in the last few years.

One is the kind of language typology outlined by Louis Hjelmslev in his last book on language where typological relationship (or affinity) among languages is defined in terms of what the late found-er of the Copenhagen school has labeled 'category function' (*kategorifunktion*) while genetic relationship in his view is based on what he has termed 'element function' or, to be more precise, the function (or correlation) of elements on the expression plane.[8] 'Category function' and 'element function' in glossematic termi-nology can, in more than one respect, be conceived as paralleling 'deep structure' and 'surface structure', respectively, as these terms are currently used in transformational generative theory.[9] It is to be hoped, incidentally, that the attempts to overcome the

---

[8] Cf. L. Hjelmslev, *Sproget: En introduktion* (Copenhagen, 1963), 88-93, esp. 92; and in the French version, *Le langage: Une introduction* (Paris, 1966), 123-129, esp. 128. For a definition of genetic relationship, see *op. cit.*, 14-34, esp. 16-17 and 33 (31-54, esp. 34-35 and 52-53, in the French edition). While this book is Hjelmslev's last publication it was actually drafted in the early 40's; cf. the editor's remarks on p. 10 of the French translation and the pertinent information in F. Whitfield's obituary in *Language* 42 (1966), 618.

[9] Cf., e.g., N. Chomsky, *Aspects of the Theory of Syntax* (Cambridge, Mass., 1965), 16-18, 64-106, 117-118, 128-147, 198-199; *Id.*, *Current Trends in Lin-guistics* III, 7-8, 33, 44-45, and elsewhere in his paper "Topics in the Theory of Generative Grammar".

metalinguistic barrier still existing between glossematic and American linguistic terminology, as undertaken several years ago by Einar Haugen and recently renewed by Sydney Lamb, will ultimately lead to a better understanding and greater appreciation of Hjelmslev's contribution to linguistic theory in those quarters of present-day American linguistics where, in spite of many a striking point of agreement, the significance of glossematics has never been properly acknowledged.[10] Genetic relationship was conceived by Hjelmslev as a process of differentiating 'continuation', transforming an underlying common linguistic structure (on the expression plane), so that, as he put it, "nous dirons donc que les éléments d'expression de chacune des langues CONTINUENT les formules communes, et que le système de chaque langue, ou chaque langue en général, CONTINUE le système total des formules communes".[11] On the other hand, his view on linguistic typology, based on his 'category' notion (both on the expression and the content plane and pertaining to 'structure' as well as 'usage', the latter distinction to some degree reminiscent of Noam Chomsky's 'competence' vs. 'performance'),[12] cultimates in this statement: "En réalité, une typologie linguistique exhaustive est la tâche la plus grande et la plus importante qui s'offre à la linguistique. Elle n'est pas, comme la génétique linguistique, régionalement limitée. En fin de compte, sa tâche est de répondre à la question: quelles structures linguistiques sont possibles, et pourquoi telles structures sont-elles possibles quand d'autres ne le sont pas? Ce faisant, elle doit, plus qu'aucune autre espèce de linguistique, s'approcher de ce qu'on pourrait

[10] Cf. E. Haugen, "Directions in Modern Linguistics", *Language* 27 (1951), 211-222; S.M. Lamb, "Epilegomena to a Theory of Language", *Romance Philology* 19 (1966), 531-573.

[11] *Op. cit.*, 53 (33, in the Danish original). The emphasis is Hjelmslev's.

[12] Cf. L. Hjelmslev, *op. cit.*, 127-128 (92 of the Danish original); on 'structure' (also 'schema' or 'pattern') in contradistinction to 'usage' in glossematic theory, see *op. cit.*, 55-69 and 131-159 (35-47 and 94-117, in the Danish edition); further also *Id.*, *Prolegomena to a Theory of Language*, rev. English ed. (Madison, 1961), 75-84; *Id.*, *Essais linguistiques* (Copenhagen, 1959), 67, and in particular, 69-81 ("Langue et parole"). On the distinction 'competence' vs. 'performance' (and its relationship to Saussure's *langue/parole* dichotomy), see, e.g., N. Chomsky, *Current Issues in Linguistic Theory* (The Hague, 1964), 23-24 and 26; *Id.*, *Aspects...*, 3-15, esp. 4, and *passim*; *Id.*, *Current Trends in Linguistics* III, 3.

appeler le problème de la nature du langage. Et, en dernier ressort, elle s'avérera hiérarchiquement supérieure à la linguistique généti- que; seule en effet elle peut permettre de comprendre les lois géné- rales selon lesquelles les langues changent et les possibilités de changement que comporte un type donné. C'est seulement par la typologie que la linguistique s'élève à des points de vue tout à fait généraux et devient une science."[13]

In a recent study on structural linguistic typology, B.A. Uspenskij, a student of Hjelmslev's, has amplified and to some degree formal- ized some of the ideas sketched in an informal and popularized fashion by the Danish linguist (his book being written with the average, non-specialized reader in mind).[14] In his study, Uspenskij introduces the notion of a METALINGUISTIC MODEL (or 'étalon lan- guage', *jazyk-ètalon*) as a tool for typological language confronta- tion. Such a metalanguage is defined as an abstract model which is used as a standard in contrastive analysis of languages on one or several levels of grammar (in the broad sense). It is suggested that the degree of typological resemblance between languages be measured in some exact terms of their respective proximity to, or, conversely, deviational distance from, this adopted metalinguistic model. The degree of proximity or deviation to be used as a typological index can be formulated by means of a set of trans- formational rules mapping the semantically interpreted deep struc- ture (or a fragment thereof) underlying a given natural language onto phonetically interpreted surface structures and correlating the found deep structure with the generalized structure (or sub- structure, respectively) of the abstract 'étalon language'. As follows from this reasoning, deep structure (of a particular language) is

[13] *Op. cit.*, 128-129 (93, in the original).
[14] Cf. B.A. Uspenskij, *Strukturnaja tipologija jazykov* (Moscow, 1965), esp. 58-68 and, for English summary, 241-242. The theoretical aspects of basing typological language classification on the concept of a metalinguistic model were explored by Uspenskij in an earlier paper, "Tipologičeskaja klassifikacija jazykov kak osnova jazykovyx sootvetstvij (Struktura jazyka-ètalona pri tipologičeskoj klassifikacii jazykov)", *Voprosy jazykoznanija* 6 (1961), 51-64. On the impact of glossematic theory on Uspenskij, cf. also his impressions reported in "Lingvističeskaja žizn' Kopengagena", *Voprosy jazykoznanija* 3 (1962), 148-151.

here conceived of as an organized system underlying a specific LANGUAGE TYPE (to be further defined) rather than underlying language per se, i.e., all language; in other words, DEEP STRUCTURE in this context carries primarily TYPOLOGICAL connotations and does not necessarily refer to any universal grammar as might be suggested by the use of this term in some recent work on transformational generative theory.[15]

Instances of implicit or explicit reference to metalinguistic models or parts of such models have been frequent in different contexts and at various stages of linguistic research. Thus, as Uspenskij points out, any statement about the presence of a certain phenomenon in a particular language implies, by itself, an indirect reference to some other language (or other languages) having the same phenomenon or, at any rate, a category of which the given phenomenon is an exponent.[16]

According to Uspenskij one has, further, to distinguish between two types of abstract metalinguistic models of the kind discussed here, a MINIMUM and a MAXIMUM type, respectively. An 'étalon language' of the minimum type is a model which, roughly speaking, amounts to the logical-algebraic (Boolean) PRODUCT of all languages typologically compared; it can therefore be defined as the underlying invariant (constant) of all these languages (at one or several levels). An 'étalon language' of the maximum type, on the other hand, can be defined as the Boolean SUM of all specific structural features of the languages involved. As a rule, it is the minimum type of abstract metalanguage that will prove to be the most powerful measure of comparison in linguistic typology.

In summary, then, a structural typology of languages is proposed

---

[15] Cf. N. Chomsky, *Aspects...*, 117-118; R. Růžička, *Studien zur Theorie der russischen Syntax* (Berlin, 1966), 19-20. Notice that I prefer 'generalized structure' to Uspenskij's 'amorphous structure' (*amorfnaja struktura*). On deep structure at a typological, rather than universal, linguistic level, see also my "Obščeslavjanskoe nasledie i inojazyčnye obrazcy v strukturnyx raznovidnostjax staroslavjanskogo predloženija", *American Contributions to the Sixth International Congress of Slavists, Prague, August 7-13, 1968*, Volume I: *Linguistic Contributions*, edited by Henry Kučera (= *Slavistic Printings and Reprintings*, 80) (The Hague, 1968), 29-64. Cf. also 26-27 and 34-48, above.

[16] See *Strukturnaja tipologija jazykov*, 60-61 and 241 (with footnotes).

to be set up by matching the generalized structure of a specially devised abstract metalinguistic model (of the minimum or, occasionally, maximum type) with the transformationally established 'infrastructures' of the respective, typologically defined natural languages under scrutiny.[17]

4. The preceding brief account for some basic principles of a new structural typology of languages, as suggested by Hjelmslev and, along similar lines, further developed by Uspenskij and others, was given here both in view of the general theoretical significance that this new approach merits, and also because its application has already begun to yield some promising concrete results. Thus, in a recent monograph on the substantive in the Balkan languages, published approximately at the same time as Uspenskij's theoretical study, the concept of an abstract, if partial, metalinguistic model devised to account for a set of shared structural features of several of the Balkan languages was introduced by T. V. Civ'jan.[18] While this is not the place to comment on the merits and shortcomings of the Soviet Balkanologist's work, as they were discussed elsewhere,[19] it is noteworthy that among the most intriguing aspects of her book are precisely the author's remarks pertaining to the possibility of establishing such a fragmentary underlying 'Balkanized' metalinguistic model which would enable us to forecast, with some degree of probability (cf. for some reservations below), a number of

---

[17] See *Strukturnaja tipologija jazykov*, 125-143 and, for English summary, 244-246; cf. also the same author's earlier study *Nekotorye voprosy strukturnoj tipologii. Avtoreferat kandidatskoj dissertacii* (Moscow, 1963), esp. 11-12. The notions of minimum and maximum types of metalinguistic models (or 'étalon languages') seem to have been first suggested by A. A. Xolodovič; cf. *Strukturnaja tipologija jazykov*, 63, fn. 21; see further *Voprosy jazykoznanija* 4 (1965), 74, with reference in fn. 1. On 'infrastructure', see above, 25-26 and 28-33.

[18] Cf. T. V. Civ'jan, *Imja suščestvitel'noe v balkanskix jazykax. K strukturno-tipologičeskoj xarakteristike balkanskogo jazykovogo sojuza* (Moscow, 1965). A preliminary study by the same author, "Opyt opisanija form novogrečeskogo suščestvitel'nogo metodom analiza i sinteza", appeared in *Voprosy jazyko-znanija* 6, (1963), 57-68.

[19] Cf. H. Birnbaum, "On Typology, Affinity, and Balkan Linguistics", *Zbornik za filologiju i lingvistiku* IX (1966), 17-30; see further my review of Civ'jan's book in *Zeitschrift für Balkanologie* IV (1966), 173-181.

future developments in the member languages of the Balkan linguistic convergence area proper, i.e., in Rumanian (including not
only Daco-Rumanian but also two of its isolated dialects, Arumanian and Megleno-Rumanian), Albanian, Modern Greek as well
as Bulgarian and Macedonian, along with the so-called Torlak (or
Prizren-Timok) dialect group of Serbo-Croatian.[20]
Consider by way of illustration the following three sentence
structures adduced by Civ'jan:

(1) Subj. + Pred. + Dir. obj. + Mod.$_{\text{dir obj}}$ + Mod.$_{\text{mod}}$
(2) Subj. + Pred. + Dir. obj. + Indir. obj. | Mod.$_{\text{indir obj}}$
(3) Subj. + Pred. + Dir. obj. + Mod.$_{\text{dir obj}}$ + Indir. obj.

In three of the Balkan languages, viz., Rumanian, Bulgarian, and
Macedonian, the syntactic relationships indicated by the above
structures can be rendered by identical or nearly identical constructions:

Rumanian: (1) *Eu dau cartea profesorului fiului meu.*
           (2) *Eu dau cartea profesorului fiului meu.*
           (3) *Eu dau cartea profesorului fiului meu.*
Bulgarian: (1) *Az davam knigata na učitelja na sina mi.*
           (2) *Az [mu] davam knigata na učitelja na sina mi.*
           (3) *Az [mu] davam knigata na učitelja na sina mi.*
Macedonian: (1) *Jas ja davam knigata na nastavnikot na moj sin.*
           (2) *Jas mu ja davam knigata na nastavnikot na moj sin.*
           (3) *Jas mu ja davam knigata na nastavnikot na moj sin.*

Except for the enclitic dative form of the personal pronoun (*mu*)
in Bulgarian (where its use is optional) and Macedonian (where it
is obligatory) in sentences number 2 and 3, it is clear that in the
mentioned Balkan languages the three semantically different mes-
sages are conveyed by means of three formally identical expressions
where any syntactic-semantic ambiguity must be resolved primarily
by the context in which each of these sentences can occur; in speech,
differences in sentence intonation can further be utilized to render
unambiguous the existing neutralization on the grammatical (mor-
phosyntactic) level. While the three quoted languages thus display

[20] Cf. Civ'jan, *op. cit.*, 158-191, esp. 183-189.

a largely uniform, generalized structure underlying these three semantically different sentences (a structure which can be considered highly typical of the Balkan convergence area), Serbo-Croatian, on the other hand, represents here the opposite, analytically simple type denoting each different syntactic relationship by a separate, non-repetitive form:

Serbo-Croatian: (1) *Ja dajem knjigu učitelja mog sina.*
(2) *Ja dajem knjigu učitelju mog sina.*
(3) *Ja dajem knjigu učitelja mom sinu.*

Albanian and Modern Greek, while not quite as strongly marked in this respect, tend toward a development in the same direction as the fully 'Balkanized' languages, Rumanian, Bulgarian, and Macedonian.[21]

It goes without saying that wherever a group of languages is characterized by an underlying generalized, largely uniform structure (definable in terms of an abstract metalinguistic model or 'étalon language' which these languages approximate to various degrees) translation from one language to another is considerably facilitated. This is precisely the situation in the Balkan convergence area.[22] It would seem a worthwhile endeavor to attempt a formal comparison of such an abstract metalinguistic model (once it has been elaborated with some degree of completeness) and the structure of some of the 'intermediate languages' as such algorithmic systems are now being devised for the purpose of machine translation.[23]

---

[21]   For further details, see T. V. Civ'jan, *op. cit.*, 184-189.

[22]   Cf. also the reasoning, with appropriate examples, in J. Ellis, *Towards a General Comparative Linguistics* (The Hague, 1966), 127-133 ("Rank-bound Translation and Areal Convergence") and 142-153 ("Possible Comparisons of Balkan and North-West European Linguistic Community, with Reference to System Reduction Method of Quantification"). In this context, H. Becker's observation, though slightly exaggerated, deserves to be quoted: "Auf dem Balkan haben sich die Sprachen so innig aneinander angepasst, dass die Hauptsprachen der Halbinsel geradezu Wort für Wort ineinander umgesetzt werden können" (*Der Sprachbund* [Berlin–Leipzig, 1948], 24).

[23]   Cf., e.g. the work on 'intermediate languages' done in MT research by I. A. Mel'čuk, Moscow, and P. Sgall, Prague.

5. If, on the one hand, we can agree with Greenberg and Jakobson that linguistic typology adds to our predictive power and if we also accept that this assumption can be corroborated by establishing various metalinguistic models (or fragments thereof) devised as a tool in typological linguistics, as suggested by Uspenskij, and, further, that such an abstract 'étalon language' can even be said to underlie the convergent development toward unification and grammatical simplicity (yielding, by and large, an increasingly analytic language structure) as in the Balkan languages (shown, with regard to the substantive, by Civ'jan), we must, on the other hand, qualify these assumptions by subscribing to the view expressed by one of the critics of Uspenskij who rightly claims that all such typological considerations have to remain more or less academic as long as the spontaneous development of language will continue to be influenced and deviated by the unpredictable, sometimes politically motivated interference of man.[24] Applied to the Balkan linguistic situation, it can thus be said that while under ideal — that is, undisturbed — conditions one may venture far-reaching predictions as to the future course of development of the languages in this area, the unpredictability of forthcoming extra-linguistic factors and events virtually invalidates and, in fact, prevents any such prophecies. While, therefore, projective prediction, based on typological or, more specifically, areal-typological considerations, for all practical purposes can at best be said to constitute a very imperfect supplementary approach to diachronic linguistics — in this case with the time dimension extending into the future and not into the past — there is of course one more fundamental difference between the range of the primary data of such prediction and that of the synchronic linguistic data used in internal reconstruction proper (in its now rather well-defined sense), as well as in the paralleling method of applying ordered (or partially ordered) generative rules. In the latter instance, that is, as regards

---

[24] Cf. Ju. V. Roždestvenskij, *Voprosy jazykoznanija* 3 (1966), 115 (in his review of Uspenskij's *Strukturnaja tipologija jazykov*); cf. also S. Klein, *Mechanical Translation* 9 (1966), 71-72 ("Prediction of Historical Events", in his article "Historical Change in Language Using Monte Carlo Techniques").

both internal reconstruction and the application of generative (phonological) rules, we have to do with data from only ONE specific language (or from some of its historically recorded or reconstructed prehistoric stages, respectively). In the case of typologically founded projective prediction, on the other hand, the very nature of a TYPOLOGICAL interpretation of synchronic data of a single language implies, in the last resort, a prior comparison or confrontation of SEVERAL languages, allowing for an initial determination and characterization in terms of typological criteria (or 'structural features') of the very language under examination.

Moreover, it must be pointed out that the method of applying a set of generative phonological rules, devised as it was with the criterion of simplicity and economy in mind,[25] and not for the specific purpose of internal reconstruction (its usefulness for the latter being rather a by-product), can in no way pretend to be a fully reliable technique for establishing relative chronology; not only does this method frequently fail to recapitulate the chain of pertinent historical events, i.e., of individual sound changes, in a correct chronological order, but it is also true that not all the input forms (or 'protoforms') suggested by the application of such (at least partially) ordered rules necessarily correspond to those original forms or, rather, sound sequences that can be posited on the basis of internal — and, for that matter, comparative — reconstruction. Examples of such discrepancies, both as regards chronological order and input forms, can be found, for instance, in T. M. Lightner's by and large quite intriguing work on the morphophonemic alternations of present-day Polish.[26] Thus, e.g., the input forms for contemporary Polish *mięs*, *rąk* (gen. pl. of *mięso* 'meat, flesh', *ręka* 'hand, arm') are set up by Lightner as *mENŝ* + *oŝ*,

---

[25] Cf., in particular, M. Halle, "On the Role of Simplicity in Linguistic Descriptions", see further also *Id.*, "Phonology in Generative Grammar" (for full references, see fn. 3, above). Lately, the earlier claimed overall usefulness of applying generative phonological rules for establishing relative chronology seems to have been somewhat deemphasized (M. Halle, personal communication).

[26] Cf. T. M. Lightner, "Preliminary Remarks on the Morphophonemic Component of Polish", esp. 226 (for full reference, see fn. 3, above).

rONk + *oŝ* (his examples no. 2 and 5), although comparative (Indo-European) evidence here suggests endings in *-õm* (*-o* + *õm* > *-õm*, *-ā* + *õm* > *-ãm* or *-õm*) or, in view of early Slavic (Old Church Slavic, etc.) -ъ, possibly *-om*, but certainly not a desinence in *-s* (Lightner's -ŝ).[27] Likewise, along with many an instance where relative chronology (as established by means of internal or comparative reconstruction, but also as evidenced by attested language evolution) coincides with the order in which generative phonological rules must be applied for the purpose of yielding, ultimately, observable morphophonemic alternations, counter-examples disputing the validity of the claimed parallelism can, no doubt, be found.[28]

A refined method of internal reconstruction does, on the other hand, seem to allow for some diachronic insights and interpretations, with reference to relative chronology as well as to identification or, rather, 'superimposition' of related linguistic models (i.e., largely, phonological and/or morphological systems), earlier not attainable by means of a more traditional approach. As an example, one could refer to the view expounded, if only in a somewhat sketchy manner, by V. V. Ivanov and V. N. Toporov and arrived at on the basis of strictly internal considerations, viz., that the (earliest) Protoslavic linguistic model — fragmentary as its reconstruction must be — is derivable from its hypothetic Protobaltic counterpart while a reverse deduction can be shown to be virtually inconceivable.[29] This, then, emphasizes once more the great significance that should be attributed to Baltic linguistic data in all and any attempts to reconstruct the earliest phase of Protoslavic.[30]

[27] For the reconstruction of the original Indo-European genitive plural ending, cf., e.g., H. Krahe, *Indogermanische Sprachwissenschaft* II, 3rd rev. ed. (Berlin, 1959), 26-27. Other reconstructions of this IE gen. pl. desinence are now also contemplated, esp. on the basis of Hittite evidence (oral communication by E. Hamp).

[28] For further discussion of Slavic (and Baltic) material as regards relative chronology and order of (generative) phonological rules, see my paper "Rekonstrukcja wewnętrzna..." (cf. fn. 3, above, and pp. 92-122, below).

[29] Cf. V. V. Ivanov and V. N. Toporov, "K postanovke voprosa..." (cf. fn. 2, above), esp. 303.

[30] As an eloquent testimony to this basic concept one can mention P. Arumaa's *Urslavische Grammatik* I (Heidelberg, 1964) (further parts forthcoming). For

It can safely be said that the role played by Slavic linguistic evidence for the reconstruction of a Common Baltic protolanguage, if indeed the actual existence of any such protolanguage can be demonstrated, will never be of any even remotely comparable magnitude.[31]

6. Finally, there exist, of course, instances where a divergent linguistic development (evolving from one parent language) results in a number of separate, though closely related languages which at some later time can be subject to a contrary, i.e., convergent, tendency, often triggered or imposed by some extra-linguistic, e.g., political, factors and leading to what could be termed a rapprochement, if not, ultimately, to a full merging of these languages descendent from a common protolanguage. As a point in case, let us refer to the linguistic situation in Scandinavia where in the nineteenth and partly also in the twentieth century attempts have been (and, are being) made to create some sort of a general 'Pannordic' (*samnordisk*) language or, rather, a metalanguage enabling the speakers of the different Scandinavian languages (at any rate, the Swedes, the Danes, and the Norwegians) to overcome any existing difficulties of inter-Scandinavian verbal communication. In effect, this skeleton of a 'Pannordic' metalanguage is made up largely by the word stock and grammatical structure shared by the three main Scandinavian languages (though allowing for a certain amount of phonological variation), focusing on particular elements only where these languages disagree to the extent of a breakdown in communication; so, e.g., in the case of the numerals where the old-fashioned numeral system of Danish is superseded by that of the other Scandinavian languages; or when secondary semantic splits which have led to a differentiation in meaning of originally single lexical items are being obliterated (such as, e.g., Danish *dreng* 'boy', Swedish *dräng* 'farmhand', Danish *pige* 'girl', Swedish

---

a detailed evaluation of Arumaa's work, see my review in *International Journal of Slavic Linguistics and Poetics* X (1966), 165-178.

[31] For some of the difficulties of reconstructing Protobaltic, see my aforementioned paper "Rekonstrukcja wewnętrzna ..." (cf. fn. 3, above; the revised English version, see pp. 92-122, below).

piga 'servant girl', Norwegian *kjole* 'evening dress, tails; gown', Swedish *kjol* 'skirt', and a number of other so-called 'dangerous words'). However, this supranational 'language', although emphasizing the common component of all the Scandinavian languages, is not particularly reminiscent of the Protonordic (*urnordisk*) parent language which, incidentally, need not to be altogether reconstructed theoretically as some fragments of it are attested by a number of Runic inscriptions. Thus, taking into account both the intervening phonological evolution, the grammatical reshaping, the conceptual increase of lexical items, and the foreign impact on the vocabulary of most Scandinavian languages,[32] the early phase of a divergent North Germanic language development (i.e., late Protonordic of the seventh through tenth centuries) and the approaching of a considerable convergence among the Scandinavian languages (i.e., 'Pannordic' of the nineteenth and twentieth centuries) need certainly not be in any one-to-one correlation. In other words, it should not be conceived of as derivable in terms of structural features (in the sense of 'Pannordic' linguistic structure being directly deducible from that of Protonordic). What this suggests, then, is that an abstract metalinguistic model, as it could partly be devised for the genetically closely related modern Scandinavian languages, could not simply be based on the Protonordic language from which they all have developed.

Similar considerations come to mind as regards the directed language planning now in progress in Norway and aiming at merging two different Scandinavian languages, the 'bookish language' (*bokmål*, earlier called *riksmål*) which is largely an adaptation of Danish to a set of Norwegian linguistic standards, and the generalized type of indigenous 'New Norwegian' of dialectal origin (*nynorsk*, earlier called *landsmål*), introduced by Ivar Aasen in the middle of the last century.[33]

[32] It has been claimed, for example, that more than half of the lexical items of present-day Swedish are of Middle Low German origin; cf. E. Wessén, *Om det tyska inflytandet på svenskt språk under medeltiden* (Stockholm, 1954), esp. 45.

[33] Cf. E. Haugen, *Language Conflict and Language Planning: The Case of Modern Norwegian* (Cambridge, Mass., 1966); *Id.*, "Linguistics and Language

What here has been said about some aspects of the divergent-convergent language situation in Scandinavia was mentioned merely to substantiate the contention that protolanguages cannot, without further qualification, be used as a suitable basis for establishing underlying metalinguistic models ('étalon languages') even in convergence areas where the languages involved are genetically related.

7. In conclusion, the preceding considerations could be summarized as follows: The two main aspects of diachrony, viz., the inquiry into the past and into the future of language evolution, can undoubtedly be viewed as two correlative approaches to the same basic phenomenon of time-determined linguistic change. In this sense, then, there is a correlation between genetic linguistics, concerned primarily with reconstructing lost protolanguages and studying language relationship and divergence, and typological linguistics, in particular, areal-typological linguistics, focusing on problems of language affinity and convergence areas and rendering possible, to some degree, prediction of future language developments. Once this general and, to be sure, widely neglected correlation of approaches to diachronic linguistics has been established (suggesting, incidentally, that any persisting equalization of diachronic and historical linguistics be abolished, the former commanding a wider range of perspectives), it is necessary, however, to state also the limitations and qualifications of such a correlation. Thus, while reconstruction and prediction and, specifically, internal reconstruction and projective prediction, both based on the evidence of synchronic data, can be viewed as two correlative sets of techniques and procedures to penetrate into the unknown spheres of linguistic evolution — one preceding, the other yet to follow the directly observable change of linguistic structure — it would imply a gross oversimplification to consider reconstruction and prediction merely

---

Planning", *Sociolinguistics. Proceedings of the UCLA Sociolinguistics Conference*, 1964, W. Bright (ed.) (The Hague–Paris, 1966), 50-71 (with discussion); *Id.*, "Semicommunication: The Language Gap in Scandinavia", *Sociological Inquiry* 36 (1966), 280-297.

reversible methods of diachronic linguistic research. Friedrich Schlegel's suggestive comparison of the historian and the prophet, referred to at the outset of this paper, is therefore not to be taken quite literally. Much of the above discussion was intended to reveal at least a few of the complexities and inherent counter-arguments that can be adduced against any such oversimplification.[34]

---

[34] For some general considerations similar to those put forward in this article (though applied to linguistic data of a different kind), see now also E. Pulgram's paper "Trends and Predictions" in *To Honor Roman Jakobson* II (The Hague–Paris, 1967), 1634-1649.

INTERNAL RECONSTRUCTION, ORDER OF SYNCHRONIC RULES IN GENERATIVE GRAMMAR, AND THE PROBLEM OF EARLY BALTO-SLAVIC RELATIONS

1. As is well known, several definitions of the method of internal reconstruction have been proposed, each differing in respect to the scope of this method's applicability.[1] T. Milewski, for example, in his last text on general linguistics characterized it as follows: "The

[1] Cf., for example, also our statement (*Ancient Indo-European Dialects*, H. Birnbaum and J. Puhvel [eds.], [Berkeley–Los Angeles, 1966], 153); "Some confusion seems still to prevail as to the scope of internal reconstruction of lost parental languages as opposed to comparative reconstruction of such languages. Thus, in the case of C[ommon]Sl[avic], some scholars would label 'internal' all reconstruction derived from the attested individual Slavic languages, reserving 'comparative' to reconstruction based on comparison with non-Slavic I[ndo-]E[uropean] languages (Baltic, Indo-Iranian, etc.), while other linguists would rather limit the use of the term 'internal' to such reconstruction deducible from the evidence of one single (in this case, Slavic) language only." Here we would now add that when it comes to reconstructing Common Slavic exclusively on the basis of data furnished by the Slavic languages themselves, we ought to differentiate between at least two major evolutionary phases of this reconstructed protolanguage — namely, between an Early Common Slavic (or Proto-Slavic) and a Late Common Slavic period. By reconstructing Common Slavic of the late period on the basis of data from various Slavic languages, we are, no doubt, concerned not with internal but with comparative reconstruction. Subsequently, Late Common Slavic thus reconstructed can, in turn, serve as a basis for internal reconstruction of a more theoretical early Proto-Slavic linguistic model. The accuracy of Proto-Slavic, internally reconstructed in this fashion, can then be verified and inevitable gaps filled by additionally applying the method of comparative reconstruction, adducing data from other Indo-European languages, in particular, Baltic. For details of the theory of reconstructing the various phases of Common Slavic (or Proto-Slavic), see now also my paper "Zur Problematik der zeitlichen Abgrenzung des Urslavischen (Über die Relativität der Begriffe Baltoslavisch/Frühurslavisch bzw. Spätgemeinslavischer Dialekt/Ureinzelslavine)", *Zeitschrift für slavische Philologie* (forthcoming).

method of internal reconstruction (part of which is the establishment of relative chronology) is based on the presence of parallel elements in a language of a given period. By analyzing the system of that language, it ascertains which elements are older and which younger. This method exists in several variants. The first of them is based on conclusions drawn from phonological parallels. — For historical morphology investigating the evolution of the morphological system of a language, the method of exceptional forms is of particular importance. This method is founded on the assumtion that whenever we are confronted by two synonymous forms, a regular one corresponding to the normal, general morphological type of the language, and a second form which is anomalous and exceptional, then the latter of these must be considered a residual form and hence the older of the two. — Related to this method is that concerned with fading forms, implying that if of two synonyms one is receding while the other is developing, the former must be the older."[2] One may add here that this last method can be applied to the field of so-called syntactic synonymy where frequent instances of competing constructions, some becoming or about to become obsolete or unproductive, others growing in productivity, are particularly suited for the application of the method of internal reconstruction.[3] Subsequently, Milewski surveys various methods

[2] Cf. T. Milewski, *Językoznawstwo* (Warsaw, 1965), 138-139. For a general appraisal of Milewski's textbook, see my review in *Language* XLIII (1967), 751-757.

[3] Generally on syntactic synonymy and its limitations, see, for example, V.P. Suxotin, *Sintaksičeskaja sinonimika v sovremennom russkom literaturnom jazyke: Glagol'nye slovosočetanija* (Moscow, 1960), esp. the theoretical introduction (3-26); and, also based on Russian data, K. Gabka, "Zur Abgrenzung lexikalischer, morphologischer und syntaktischer Synonymie", *Zeitschrift für Slawistik* XII (1967), 727-734, with ample further references, particularly to literature treating syntactic synonymy in Russian. Cf. further T.P. Lomtev, *Očerki po istoričeskomu sintaksisu russkogo jazyka* (Moscow, 1956), 16-33 ("Istoričeskij process otmiranija èlementov starogo kačestva i nakoplenie èlementov novogo kačestva"). On methods of reconstructing unattested (preliterary) syntactic structures ('texts') on the basis of ancient Indo-European languages, see, for example, C. Watkins, "Preliminaries to the Reconstruction of Indo-European Sentence Structure", *Proceedings of the Ninth International Congress of Linguists*, H. G. Lunt (ed.), (The Hague, 1964), 1035-1045, with contributions to the discussion by H. Rosén, H. Seiler, and H. Birnbaum; V.V. Ivanov,

of historical linguistics and compares the method just referred to
with other approaches used in the recovery of linguistic developments (attested or preliterary). In particular, he compares it with:
(1) the traditional philological method, based on contrasting data
gleaned from texts of different periods; (2) the comparative method,
designed to establish the oldest among a set of linguistic elements
(such as a phoneme, morpheme, word, phrase, or clause) found in
languages which can be traced back to a common protolanguage,
and (3) historical dialectology, based on extra-linguistic, *viz.* spatial,
criteria. Specifically, this method infers from contemporary linguistic boundaries and isogloss bundles as to their former location.
As a result, Milewski concludes that "the method of internal reconstruction (relative chronology) is in general of secondary importance. It permits the positing of only a few inconsistent facts, but
precludes the possibility of reconstructing the entire evolution of
a given language."[4] Even if we agree with Milewski that instances
of unconditioned phonemic split should not be considered under
this method of internal reconstruction,[5] his rather narrow view oj

---

*Obščeindoevropejskaja, praslavjanskaja i anatolijskaja jazykovye sistemy (srav-
nitel'no-tipologičeskie očerki)* (Moscow, 1965), 185-289 ("Rekonstrukcija sin-
taksičeskix struktur", with additional references); cf. further, with particular
reference to Common Slavic data, V.V. Ivanov, V.N. Toporov, "K rekonstrukcii praslavjanskogo teksta", *Slavjanskoe jazykoznanie. Doklady sovetskoj
delegacii. V Meždunarodnyj s"ezd slavistov* (Moscow, 1963), 88-158, and, by
the same authors, *Slavjanskie jazykovye modelirujuščie semiotičeskie sistemy
(Drevnij period)* (Moscow, 1965), 218-239 ("Nekotorye fragmenty rekonstruirue-
myx slavjanskix tekstov").

[4] See *Językoznawstwo*, 149.

[5] See *Językoznawstwo*, 147. According to Milewski, the principle of unconditioned phonemic split can be formulated as follows: If two or more phonemes
of language A correspond to one phoneme of language B, and it is impossible
to state the conditions and causes of a split, then language A represents the
older state since the merging of several phonemes (attested in language A) into
one phoneme (of language B) is more likely to occur than the unconditioned
and unmotivated splitting of one phoneme (in language B) into several phonemes (in language A). Serbo-Croatian and Russian, in respect to the Common
Slavic reduced vowels, can serve as an example of unconditioned phonemic
split. Whereas the former language has a single reflex /a/ of these reduced
vowels in strong position (as still most clearly preserved in some Old Church
Slavic texts), the latter language shows two separate reflexes, /e/ and /o/. (Here
we are disregarding the controversial problem whether Old Russian /e/ and /o/

the applicability and potentials of this method can hardly gain unanimous acceptance.

The paper by J. Kuryłowicz, containing many new penetrating thoughts and insightful observations, which was presented at the Ninth International Congress of Linguists,[6] is a significant contribution to the methodology of internal reconstruction. His insistence, for example, that a hierarchical ordering of rewrite rules be applicable to reconstructed Indo-European morphs of the type $T_1eiT_2 \rightarrow T_1iT_2 \rightarrow T_1oiT_2$ etc. (*$leiq^u \rightarrow$ *$liq^u \rightarrow$ *$loiq^u$; *$leuk \rightarrow$ *$luk \rightarrow$ *$louk$; further, *$leiq^u \rightarrow leik\text{-}to\text{-} \rightarrow$ *$leik\text{-}t\acute{o}\text{-} \rightarrow$ *$lik\text{-}t\acute{o}\text{-}$ etc.), illustrating the mechanism of ablaut,[7] is important for our subsequent discussion as well. However, it must be said that Kuryłowicz' failure to unambiguously define the very scope of internal reconstruction elicited a few critical remarks from some of the discussants

---

— prior to the sound change /e/ > /o/ — should be considered merely allophones of one and the same phoneme /o/, implemented as /e/ after a palatalized consonantal segment and as /o/ after a nonpalatalized consonantal segment.) As shown by this example alone (where Russian, with its double reflex of strong reduced vowels, represents an older state as compared to Serbo-Croatian, with its single reflex), instances of unconditioned (spontaneous) phonemic split can be treated only in a comparative framework. In this respect, it seems difficult to subscribe to the assertion by J. Kuryłowicz that "methods of internal reconstruction have been applied in an increasing degree, more or less consciously and explicitly, by neogrammarians. Thus, e.g., they have rejected the possibility of spontaneous phonetic split..." (in his report "On the Methods of Internal Reconstruction", *Proceedings of the Ninth International Congress of Linguists*, 9). However, it is possible to explain conditioned phonemic split and the resulting morphophonemic alternations in terms of the method of internal reconstruction. Relying solely on synchronic data projected into the past (i.e., by internal reconstruction), the morphophonemic vowel-zero alternation (often marked #, i.e., $e:o/\emptyset$) of Contemporary Standard Russian, for example, can be traced back to the Common Slavic /ь/:/ъ/ alternation in strong and weak position, respectively. For additional details, with examples, cf., *inter alia*, H.M. Hoenigswald, *Language Change and Linguistic Reconstruction* (Chicago, 1959), 99-104 ("Morphophonemic Consequences of Phonemic Split: Internal Reconstruction").

[6] See J. Kuryłowicz, "On the Methods of Internal Reconstruction", *Proceedings...*, 9-36, with contributions to the discussion by Birnbaum, Bonfante, Heller, Lehmann, Rosén, Strang, and Winter).

[7] Cf. *Proceedings*, 15-16.

(Birnbaum, Hamp).[8] Only in the introductory note to the discussion which appears in the Congress Proceedings does Kuryło-wicz seek to define the particular nature of internal reconstruction as a new linguistic term, endowed with a special meaning only *a posteriori* — in other words, he contrasts it with linguistic reconstruction in the traditional sense, i.e., reconstruction utilizing data provided by the comparative method.[9] According to Kuryłowicz, we must interprete internal reconstruction as designating specifically LINGUISTIC reconstruction in contradistinction to other approaches aimed at the recovery of phenomena and processes not entirely of a linguistic nature and operating, therefore, in conjunction with extra-linguistic methods as well. Kuryłowicz points specifically to the "chronological order of the reconstructed linguistic facts (relative chronology)" as the goal of all linguistic reconstruction. Only in his reply to Hamp[10] does the distinguished Polish scholar indicate that internal reconstruction refers, in fact, to techniques and devices applied to a single language.

Here it ought to be emphasized that while relative chronologies can be established solely on the basis of strictly linguistic criteria, absolute chronologies of linguistic change can, in addition, be

---

[8]   See *Proceedings*, 32, and Kuryłowicz' reply to Hamp's remarks (*ibid.*, 36; the latter unfortunately not published in the *Proceedings*): "The term 'internal reconstruction' as used here refers to devices and procedures applied within ONE language. Internal reconstruction is a LINGUISTIC procedure since it does not have recourse to extra-linguistic considerations like physiology of speech, psychology, and so on. Reconstruction in the traditional sense (COMPARATIVE GRAMMAR OF I.-E.) has not always been purely linguistic." Our reservations, incidentally, refer to the selection of appropriate examples (based largely on the comparative method), rather than to the lack of any precise definition of the method of internal reconstruction; cf. also Kuryłowicz' definition quoted in fn. 10, below.

[9]   See *Proceedings*, 29-30.

[10]   See *Proceedings*, 36 (cf. also the quotation adduced in fn. 8, above). At the outset of his report Kuryłowicz gave a somewhat loose definition of internal reconstruction (*ibid.*, 9): "The expression 'internal reconstruction' has been used as a technical term... to denote the diachronic conclusions that may be drawn from a synchronic analysis of linguistic data without or before having recourse to comparison, linguistic geography and 'areal linguistics' and glottochronology."

constructed on other considerations which also take into account extra-linguistic, in particular social, cultural, and geographical factors. Indeed, it is data from fields such as lexical borrowing and onomastics, especially toponomastics (i.e., 'mixed' fields on the borderline of linguistics and a number of other disciplines), that often provide the clues for establishing the absolute chronology of a linguistic phenomenon or change. Perhaps, one could even differentiate between three fundamental types of reconstruction: (1) COMPARATIVE, based on a juxtaposition of both synchronic and diachronic data from two or more languages; (2) INTERNAL, based on synchronic data from only one language; and (3) EXTERNAL, based on extraneous linguistic elements (borrowings, loan and foreign words, non-native proper names, etc.). Through comparative and external reconstruction both absolute and relative chronologies can be established to a certain degree; internal reconstruction, on the other hand, will yield only relative chronologies.

Furthermore, in some recent monographs and texts treating historical (diachronic) linguistics and its methodology, much emphasis is placed on a strictly linguistic argumentation for the method of internal reconstruction. Two full chapters of H. M. Hoenigswald's book on linguistic change, for example, are devoted primarily to methodological problems of internal linguistic reconstruction.[11] Also W. P. Lehmann, when discussing the method of internal reconstruction in his, generally speaking, somewhat old-fashioned textbook of historical linguistics, illustrates this method by citing Saussure's assumption of the existence in Proto-Indo-European of consonantal elements which had subsequently disappeared. Kuryłowicz later was able to identify traces of these elements with certain sounds of Hittite (*ḫ*, *ḫḫ*), thereby laying a

---

[11] Cf. H. M. Hoeningswald *op. cit.*, 68-71 (ch. 7) and 99-111 (ch. 10); see further ch. 11 on relative chronology (112-118); also 151-158. Among articles particularly concerned with internal reconstruction, the one by W. L. Chafe, "Internal Reconstruction in Seneca", *Language* XXXV (1959), 477-495, deserves mention for it not only makes extensive reference to early treatments, but also contains, in its introduction, important theoretical considerations regarding the method itself.

solid foundation for the so-called laryngeal theory in Indo-European linguistics.[12]

Finally, attempts have also been made to apply the method of internal reconstruction to phenomena of loss in linguistic evolution, especially of lexical items. However, a precise statistical interpretation of these processes (such as that proposed by the method of glottochronology or lexicostatistics) has proven inadequate, as it was unable to withstand serious criticism.[13]

Summing up the above-mentioned (as well as some other) definitions of the scope and goals of internal reconstruction, it can be said that this method, proceeding from synchronic data of a single language (i.e., of a particular phase in the development of that language), has as its chief goal the recovery of the order or, rather, the relative chronology of a set of preceding linguistic changes (primarily phonemic and morphophonemic, but also, though to a lesser extent, morphological, syntactic, and lexical), inferrable from these data. The method of internal reconstruction appears to be indispensable in some instances, namely: (a) wherever we are dealing with a language which has neither a recorded history nor any known cognates; (b) wherever we wish to reconstruct details about a language's relatively recent past, when such data cannot be established by a comparison of that language with its predecessor (the protolanguage from which it is derived or an earlier phase of that same language); and (c) wherever we are concerned with reconstructing the development or a specific earlier

[12] See W.P. Lehmann, *Historical Linguistics: an Introduction* (New York, 1962), 99-106 (ch. 6: "The Method of Internal Reconstruction"), esp. 101-102; cf. also 239. J. Kuryłowicz' discovery was first published in his article "ə indoeuropéen et ḫ hittite", *Symbolae grammaticae in honorem J. Rozwadowski* I (Cracow, 1927), 95-104; and subsequently in greater detail in his *Études indoeuropéennes* I (= *PAU PKJ* 21), (Cracow, 1935), 27-76 ("II. Sur les éléments consonantiques disparus en indoeuropéen"); cf. also his note "A propos de hittite ḫ: Réponse à une critique de M.W. Petersen", *BSL* XXXVI (1935), 25-27.
[13] Cf. W.P. Lehmann, *Historical Linguistics*, 107-113 (with bibliographical references). For a critique of the method of glottochronology, see, among other things, I. Fodor, *The Rate of Linguistic Change: Limits of the Application of Mathematical Methods in Linguistics* (The Hague, 1965), *passim* (with references).

stage of a protolanguage (the last evolutionary phase of which can be recovered by means of the comparative method as applied to the daughter languages of that protolanguage). In other cases, internal reconstruction can provide an important supplement, allowing for the corroboration of reconstructions arrived at by the comparative method and other techniques of historical linguistics.[14]

2. In recent years attention has been focused on the alleged parallelism obtaining between the order of linguistic change as established by relative chronology (by means of internal reconstruction) and an order of a different kind, namely that of applying phonological (or, in traditional terms, morphophonemic) rules devised by generative grammar. Observations regarding such a suggested parallelism can be found, in particular, in work by American linguists of the M.I.T. school and by some of their followers, including certain Soviet linguists.[15] As is well known, however, it has long

[14] A situation such as that described under (c) obtains precisely in the reconstruction of Common Slavic; cf. also fn. 1, above. For some concrete examples of applying the method of internal reconstruction to Common Slavic, see, for instance, G.Y. Shevelov, *A Prehistory of Slavic: The Historical Phonology of Common Slavic* (Heidelberg, 1964, and New York, 1965), *passim*. Concerning the methods of reconstruction — comparative, internal and, in addition, 'integrated comparative', advocated by the author — see esp. 3-11; cf. also the criticism by J. Van Campen, "On the Appearance of a New Work on Common Slavic Phonology (A Review Article)", *International Journal of Slavic Linguistics and Poetics* X (1966), 52-81, and further also the review by A. Vaillant, *BSL* LX: 2 (1965), 124-127. Further, cf. C.L. Ebeling, "Questions of Relative Chronology in Common Slavic and Russian Phonology", *Dutch Contributions to the Fifth International Congress of Slavicists* (The Hague, 1963), 27-42, esp. 31-38. The above definition of the scope and chief goals of the method of internal reconstruction coincides roughly with that by W.L. Chafe in *Language* XXXV (1959), 478 (see fn. 11, above).

[15] Cf. in particular some of the articles by M. Halle; "On the Role of Simplicity in Linguistic Descriptions", *Structure of Language and its Mathematical Aspects. Proceedings of the Twelfth Symposium in Applied Mathematics*, R. Jakobson (ed.), (Providence, R.I., 1961), 89-94, esp. 92-94 (using by way of illustration the relative chronology established between Grimm's and Verner's Laws in Germanic); *Id.*, "Phonology in Generative Grammar", *Linguistic Essays: On the Occasion of the Ninth International Congress of Linguists* (*LCNY*, *Publications* 4 = *Word* XVIII, 1-2), (New York, 1962), 54-72, esp. 66-72 (republished with slight modifications in *The Structure of Language. Readings*

been acknowledged that rules of synchronic descriptive grammar (in particular at the morphophonemic level) frequently mirror diachronic, primarily phonological, changes which a language has earlier undergone. Thus, among American linguists, for example, this fact was recognized and discussed already by L. Bloomfield and E. Sapir.[16]

---

in the Philosophy of Language, J. A. Fodor, J. J. Katz (eds.), (Englewood Cliffs, N.J., 1964), 334-352, esp. 346-352; *Id.*, "O pravilax russkogo sprjaženija", *American Contributions to the Fifth International Congress of Slavists*, Vol I: *Linguistic Contributions* (The Hague, 1963), 113-132, esp. 127. Cf. further also the articles by T. M. Lightner: "Preliminary Remarks on the Morphophonemic Component of Polish", M.I.T. Research Laboratory of Electronics, *Quarterly Progress Report* 71 (1963), 220-235 (where the author derives some 65-67 forms of Contemporary Standard Polish from their Early Common Slavic prototypes by means of a total of 51 phonological rules; *Id.*, "O cikličeskix pravilax v russkom sprjaženii", *Voprosy jazykoznanija* 2 (1965), 45-54, esp. 51-54 (further developing some of Halle's ideas)'; *Id.*, "On the Phonology of the Old Church Slavonic Conjugation", *IJSLP* X (1966), 1-28; and some other contributions by the same author. Of Soviet linguists this problem has been treated by, among others, A. A. Zaliznjak in "O vozmožnoj svjazi meždu operacionnymi ponjatijami sinxronnogo opisanija i diaxroniej", *Simpozium po strukturnomu izučeniju znakovyx sistem* (Moscow, 1962) (not available for page reference), and in "Sinxronnoe opisanie i vnutrennjaja rekonstrukcija", *Problemy sravnitel'- noj grammatiki indoevropejskix jazykov. Naučnaja sessija. Tezisy dokladov* (Moscow, 1964), 51-54. Reference to the alleged parallelism is also made by N. Chomsky, *Current Trends in Linguistics* III (The Hague–Paris, 1966), 57 (in his contribution "Topics in the Theory of Generative Grammar", now also available separately); E. S. Klima, "Relatedness between Grammatical Systems", *Language* XL (1964), 1-20, esp. 2; S. Saporta, "Ordered Rules, Dialect Differences and Historical Processes", *Language* XLI (1965), 218-224; B. Sigurd, "Generative Grammar and Historical Linguistics", *Acta Linguistica Hafniensia* X (1966), 35-48; N. E. Enkvist, "Tre modeller för ljudhistorisk forskning", *Soc. Scient. Fenn.* XLIV B, 4 (1966); B. Malmberg, *Actes du Xᵉ Congrès international des linguistes, I* (Bucharest, 1969), 17. For a critique of the concept of this parallelism by V. J. Zeps, based on the same data as partially used in this article, see below. For a recent discussion of the two basic approaches to linguistic reconstruction (internal and comparative), illustrated by Balto-Finnic (Finnish and Lapp) data, see also R. Anttila, "The Relation between Internal Reconstruction and the Comparative Method", *Ural-Altaische Jahrbücher* 40: 3-4 (1968), 159-173. While claiming "the complete identity of the mechanisms of phonemic analysis, the comparative method, and internal reconstruction (morphophonemic analysis)", the common mechanism being labeled 'contrasting mechanism', Anttila concludes "that historical and descriptive linguistics support each other".

[16]   Cf. T. M. Lightner, *IJSLP* X (1966), 24, fn. 39 (with references).

5ı 2.2.0

Here, to illustrate such a parallelism in the order of rules we might first consider a few simple examples quoted by A. Zaliznjak.[17] As suggested by the Soviet linguist, the two sets of Russian words *tigr, tígry, tigríca* and *volk, vólki, volčíca,* could be said to correspond to each other in a one-to-one relationship, except that two phonological rewrite rules — (1) $ki \rightarrow či$, and (2) $ky \rightarrow ki$ — have to be applied (in this order) to the second set of words, which therefore can be theoretically represented by the underlying forms *volk,* **vólky, *volkíca.* Thus, applying these rules, we derive *volk,* **vólky, *volkíca → volk, *vólky, volčíca → volk, vólki, volčíca.* The order of the two phases, (1) $ki \rightarrow či$ and (2) $ky \rightarrow ki$ corresponds, as we know, to the chronological relationship of Common Slavic and Old Russian (12th-13th cc.), respectively.[18]

The second example is taken from Latvian. To explain the differentiated forms of the present singular of the verbs represented by the infinitives *mest, jaust, cept, kāpt, viz.*:

	I	II	III	IV
1sg	metu	jaušu	cepu	kāpju
2sg	met	jaut	cep	kāp
3sg	met	jauš	cep	kāpj

one may proceed from a uniform set of verbal endings, 1sg -*u*, 2sg -*x*, 3sg -*Ø*, which are added to the four stems: I *met-,* II *jautj-,* III *cep-,* IV *kāpj-.* Applying the smallest possible — i.e., the most

---

[17] Cf. A.A. Zaliznjak, "Sinxronnoe opisanie i vnutrennjaja rekonstrukcija"' *Problemy...,* 51-52.

[18] Cf. G.Y. Shevelov, *op. cit.,* 249-263; V.I. Borkovskij and P.S. Kuznecov, *Istoričeskaja grammatika russkogo jazyka,* 2nd ed. (Moscow, 1965), 129 (paragraph 88); V. Kiparsky, *Russische historische Grammatik* I (Heidelberg, 1963), 135-136 and 153. — While even the example just quoted shows the correspondence between the application of ordered synchronic rules and the chronology of sound change, it should, however, be pointed out that the intermediary set of forms (*volk, *vólky, volčíca*) does not reflect any actual stage of Common Slavic. In Late Common Slavic these forms were *vьlkъ, vьlci, vьlčíca;* Proto-Russian, *vьlkъ, vьlci, vьlčíca.* (The change $c > k$ in the nominative plural is owing to analogical leveling in Early Old Russian; the substitution of the original accusative plural for the nominative plural ending did not occur in Old Russian until the 13th-14th cc.; cf. V.I. Borkovskij, P.S. Kuznecov, *op. cit.,* 183 and 215-217).

economical — number of phonological rules, (1) $jx \to x$, (2) $x \to$ $\varnothing$, (3) $tj \to š$, we can reconstruct the following evolutionary phases:

0. INPUT

	I	II	III	IV
1sg	*met-u	*jautj-u	*cep-u	*kāpj-u
2sg	*met-x	*jautj-x	*cep-x	*kāpj-x
3sg	*met-Ø	*jautj-Ø	*cep-Ø	*kāpj-Ø

1. $jx \to x$:

	I	II	III	IV
1sg	*met-u	*jautj-u	*cep-u	*kāpj-u
2sg	*met-x	*jautj-x →	*cep-x	*kāpj-x →
		*jaut-x		*kāp-x
3sg	*met-Ø	*jautj-Ø	*cep-Ø	*kāpj-Ø

2. $x \to \varnothing$:

	I	II	III	IV
1sg	*met-u	*jautj-u	*cep-u	*kāpj-u
2sg	*met-x →	*jaut-x →	*cep-x →	*kāp-x →
	*met-Ø	*jaut-Ø	*cep-Ø	*kāp-Ø
3sg	*met-Ø	*jautj-Ø	*cep-Ø	*kāpj-Ø

3. $tj \to š$:

	I	II	III	IV
1sg	*met-u	*jautj-u →	*cep-u	*kāpj-u
	(= metu)	*jauš-u	(= cepu)	(= kāpju)
		(= jaušu)		
2sg	*met-Ø	*jaut-Ø	*cep-Ø	*kāp-Ø
	(= met)	(= jaut)	(= cep)	(= kāp)
3sg	*met-Ø	*jautj-Ø →	*cep-Ø	*kāpj-Ø
	(= met)	*jauš-Ø	(= cep)	(= kāpj)
		(= jauš)		

In view of the many unknown factors in reconstructing the development of Proto-Baltic and East Common Baltic (i.e., the immediate predecessor of Lithuanian and Latvian) as well as of Proto-Latvian (i.e., of a separate preliterary Latvian language prior to its earliest attestation toward the end of the 16th century), it seems somewhat difficult to demonstrate any parallelism between the application of ordered synchronic rules (of generative phonology) and the relative chronology of the covert sound changes resulting in the modern Latvian forms (slightly simplified here for our purposes).[19] The situation in Slavic, on the other hand, lends itself better to testing the validity of such a claimed parallelism and, therefore, a further example from that language group may here be appropriate.

A case in point is provided, on the one hand, by the relative chronology of the Common Slavic palatalizations of velars and, on the other, by the application of ordered phonological rules to a set of paradigmatically linked words of one language showing the *k* / *č* / *c* alternation. While alternations of this kind have persisted into modern times in some of the Slavic languages (such as Polish, Ukrainian, and Belorussian), the examples to be quoted below are from Old Church Slavic, the oldest recorded Slavic language, which, in terms of these alternations, represents by and large Late Common Slavic. (Late Common Slavic, reconstructed on the basis of comparative data, can serve as a point of departure for further, internal reconstruction of the preceding evolutionary phases of Proto-Slavic; cf. fn. 1, with references.)

Let us therefore consider four case forms (nominative, vocative, locative singular, and nominative plural) of two old Church Slavic masculine nouns of the so-called hard-stem declension (historically *o*-stems): *rabъ, rabe, rabě, rabi* and *člověkъ, člověče, člověcě, člověci*. The second set of forms can be considered to fully match

---

[19] Concerning the difficulties in reconstructing the preliterary stages of the Baltic languages, as well as Proto-Baltic, see, for example, V. V. Ivanov and V. N. Toporov, "O postanovke voprosa o drevnejšix otnošenijax baltijskix i slavjanskix jazykov", *Issledovanija po slavjanskomu jazykoznaniju* (Moscow, 1961), 273-305, esp. 276; cf. further also section 3 (numbered 5) on Balto-Slavic in my article "Zur Problematik ...", to appear in *ZfslPh*, quoted in fn. 1, above, as well as my contribution "Four Approaches to Balto-Slavic", in *Donum Balticum* (*Festschrift for Chr. S. Stang*, forthcoming). For details of the historical development of Latvian, cf. in particular the textbooks and monographs by J. Endzelin (see the bibliographical data in the volumes published in honor of his 85th birthday, *Rakstu krājums veltijums ... Jānim Endzelīnam ...* [Riga, 1959], 659-701, and *In honorem Endzelini* [Chicago, 1960], 1-24. His two works, *Lettische Grammatik* [Riga, 1922], and *Latviešu valodas gramatika* [Riga, 1951], are particularly fundamental). The above-quoted simplified Latvian forms are cited here (and in Zaliznjak's article) without taking into account differences in intonation, parallel forms, the distinction between *e* and *ę*, etc. For details, see J. Endzelin, *Lettische Grammatik*, 122 (*kâpj:kâp*), 549 (*męt*), 601 (*jàušu*), 606 (*kâpju*), 733 (paradigm of present indicative), and *passim*.

the first, except that it has been modified by the application of two phonological rules: (1) *ke* → *če*, and (2) *kě, ki* → *cě, ci*.[20] Prior to the application of these rules, the second set could be represented in a 'pre-rewrite' form as follows: *člověkъ, *člověke, *člověkě, *člověki*, yielding (after application of rule 1) *člověkъ, člověče, *člověkě, *člověki* and, subsequently (after application of rule 2), *člověkъ, člověče, člověcě, člověci*. The order of application of these two synchronic rules corresponds, as we know, to the relative chronology of the Common Slavic regressive palatalizations of velars.[21]

Things turn out to be much more complicated, however, when we include in our considerations noun forms showing the results of the so-called progressive (or Baudouin) palatalization of velars. This holds true regarding both the chronology of this palatalization in relation to the first (regressive) palatalization (of the type *k* > *č* before original front vowels) and also in relation to the second regressive palatalization (of the type *k* > *c* or, rather, originally *k* > *c'* before secondary front vowels derived from earlier diph-

[20] Here we are ignoring possible prosodic differences not indicated in Old Church Slavic. The fact that rule 2 applies only if *ě* and *i* are secondary (i.e., are derived from the original diphthongs *oi* and *ai* which can be assumed to have existed in Early Proto-Slavic) need not be taken into consideration here since -*ě*, -*i* as primary front vowels (i.e., representing earlier *ē, ī, ei*) are not found as desinences in the paradigm of this declension (*o*-stems).

[21] It should be remembered, however, that some of the above 'pre-rewrite' forms are merely to be considered as abstractions, and not as corresponding to any actual forms that can be assumed to have existed in a given period. Thus, for example, a form *člověke* never did actually exist for the change *ke* → *če* (i.e., rule 1) was only part of a more general Common Slavic sound change, *k* > *č* before all original front vowels, that is to say, the first palatalization of velars. Thus, for the earliest period of Proto-Slavic, or even for Balto-Slavic, we must posit a form *kelovoike* or *kelavaike*; cf. L. Sadnik and R. Aitzetmüller, *Handwörterbuch zu den altkirchenslavischen Texten* (Heidelberg–The Hague, 1955), 223 (entry 116), and R. Trautmann, *Baltisch-Slavisches Wörterbuch* (Göttingen, 1923), 339 (second entry *sub ɥaika-*). As to the difficulties in specifying the quality of the original diphthong (*oi* or, perhaps more likely, *ai*), cf. also P. Arumaa, *Urslavische Grammatik*, I (Heidelberg, 1964), 85. — Likewise, it seems at least doubtful that forms of the type *člověkě, *člověki* ever really existed. Rather, the monophthongization *oi* (*ai*) > *ě*, -*i* was immediately followed by, or concomitant with, a change in articulation of the velars *k, g, x* towards originally palatalized dental affricates and fricatives, respectively.

thongs). The result of this latter softening is basically the same as that of the progressive (Baudouin) palatalization. Without even entering into a discussion of the still highly controversial question of chronological order between the progressive and the second regressive palatalizations (cf. below), let us, for the time being, only consider the problem of relative chronology between the first (regressive) and the progressive palatalizations.[22] The two sets of words, *človĕkъ, človĕče* (*človĕcĕ, človĕci*) and *otьcь, otьče* (*otьci, otьci*) may here illustrate this problem. It is usually assumed in textbooks and taught in the classroom that only the form of the vocative (*otьče*) indicates the fact that words of the type *otьcь* were originally inflected as hard stems (in -*o*) prior to the effect of the progressive palatalization: *otьcь* < *otьkъ, gen. sg. *otьka, etc.[23] By applying the two rules, (1) *ke → če*, (2) *ьk → ьc*, this could be reformulated as follows: *človĕkъ*, *človĕke : *otьkъ, **otьke → človĕkъ, človĕče* : **otьkъ, otьče → človĕkъ, človĕče* : *otьcь, otьče*.[24]

---

[22] The progressive (Baudouin) palatalization, considered by most specialists the third Common Slavic palatalization of velars, was, according to the opinion of some Slavists, not the third, but actually the second palatalization. Cf., among others, K. Knutsson, *Über die sogenannte zweite Palatalisierung in den slavischen Sprachen* (Lund, 1926); R. Ekblom, *Die frühe dorsale Palatalisierung im Slavischen* (Uppsala, 1951); and F.V. Mareš, *The Origin of the Slavic Phonological System and Its Development up to the End of Slavic Language Unity* (= *Michigan Slavic Materials* 6) (Ann Arbor, 1965), 33-57. For a discussion of the absolute as well as relative chronology of the progressive palatalization of velars, see now also G.Y. Shevelov, *A Prehistory of Slavic*, 338-363 (with further references, 362-363), esp. 349-354. Most recently, the problem of the relevant conditions and chronology was thoroughly discussed, with ample reference to previous treatments, by M. Jeżowa, *Z problemów tak zwanej trzeciej palatalizacji tylnojęzykowych w językach słowiańskich* (= *Kom. Słowianozn. PAN, Monogr. Slawist.*, 130) (Wrocław–Warsaw–Cracow, 1968), esp. 7-51. See now further also J. Hamm, 'Die Verschiebung der Velarkonsonanten', *Wien. slavist. Jb.* XV (1969), 38-58.

[23] See, for example, G.Y. Shevelov, *A Prehistory of Slavic*, 348 and 352.

[24] Strictly speaking, the second rule would have to be formulated somewhat differently: *ьkъ → ьcь* or, generalizing, "*ьk → ьc* with a concomitant, automatic change of the following back vowel to its front counterpart (*ъ > ь, y > i, o > e, ǫ > ę*) except for *u* and *a* and the — morphological rather than phonological — change *ĕ > i*." (The exceptions of *u* and *a* need to be mentioned only if we do not interpret the changes *u > 'u* and *a > 'a* phonemically as a shift from the back to the front series of vowels, i.e., /u/ > /ü/, /a/ > /ä/, as

When formulating and applying such phonological rules, however, we are basically going beyond the synchronic data of Old Church Slavic. For utilizing only data of that language (or, for that matter, any other Slavic language, ancient or modern), we would have to start out from a number of postulates suggested either by certain linguistic universals or by our knowledge of some specific earlier processes in the evolution of that language which cannot be derived from the synchrony of a single language (here, Old Church Slavic). Compare, for example, the chronologically different origins of OCS ě, i. These postulates could include, among other things, the following statements:

1. The point of departure is the contrast of Old Church Slavic forms of the type otьcь (nom. sg.) vs. otьče (voc. sg.).

2. There is nothing in the phonological system of Old Church Slavic that would prevent us from assuming the existence of such forms as otьčь or *otьce.[25] (In other words, the Old Church Slavic affricates č and c are not allophones of one phoneme, i.e., they are not in syntagmatic complementary distribution.)

3. We cannot, therefore, posit a change otьčь > otьcь or *otьce > otьče; rather, we must presume that both forms (otьcь as well as otьče) can be derived from a common root *otьX- (X here symbolizing a consonant as yet unidentified.) On the basis of comparison with other Old Church Slavic forms showing the morphophenemic alternations of the type k : č : c (e.g., člověkъ, člověče člověcě, člověci :: *otьX- : otьče : otьci, otьci), we can infer that the unidentified consonant (X) must have been k, thus, *otьk-.

4. We can reconstruct the theoretical forms *otьkъ, *otьke as

---

is now frequently done.) Alternatively, rule 2 could be devided into two subrules: (2a) ьk → ьc', (2b) c'ъ, c'y, c'o, c'ǫ, c'ě → c'ъ, c'i, c'e, c'ę, c'i.

[25] The form otьčь, though of different origin (< *otьkjь), is, incidentally, attested as a possessive adjective in Old Church Slavic; cf. L. Sadnik and R. Aitzetmüller, Handwörterbuch, 79, s. v. The sound sequence otьce- is also found, though not as a separate word, but merely as part of a longer unit, namely in certain flectional forms (instr. sg., dat.-instr. dual, dat. pl.) of the noun otьcь.

underlying the attested forms *otьcь, otьče*, positing the nominative ending (-ъ) on the basis of other nominative forms of the masculine hard-stem declension. A form such as **otьkъ* could not be posited since the sequence *k* + *ь*, being replaced by *č* + *ь*, already in the Common Slavic period, was inadmissible in Old Church Slavic; (cf. *kъ-to* : *čь-to* < **kʷo-* : **kʷi-*, etc.). However, the attested nominative singular form is *otьcь*, not **otьčь* (for the adjectival form, see fn. 25). As for the vocative **otьke* > *otьče*, the final vowel does not present any particular problem.

5. Since forms of the type *otьčь* and **otьce* do not violate the phonological system of Old Church Slavic (cf. *sub* 2, above), one can assume that the actually attested forms *otьcь, otьče* must have been derived from **otьkъ, *otьke* at different periods.

6. HYPOTHESIS I: The change *k* > *c* (*c'*) occurred prior to the change *k* > *č*. Assuming such a chronology, however, the emergence of the form *otьče* would remain unexplained, since it could not have developed from **otьke* through an intermediate stage **otьce* as this latter form, being phonologically acceptable, would need no further modification (cf. *sub* 2, above).

7. MODIFIED HYPOTHESIS IA: The change *k* > *c* (*c'*), though preceding the change *k* > *č*, did not occur before *e* since forms of the type *otьče* can be derived only directly from **otьke* (cf. *sub* 4 and 6, above). In this case, however, those forms which show progressive palatalization and have *e* after the affricate or fricative element remain unexplained (cf. instr. sg. *otьcemь*, dat.-instr. dual *otьcema*, dat. pl. *otьcemъ*; cf. also, for example, *lice* and other words in *ce*; see *sub* 2, above). The even more far-reaching and, in fact, unreasonable assumption that the change *k* > *c* (*c'*) did not occur at all before front vowels can be discarded simply on the evidence of other inflectional forms of *otьcь* (loc. sg. *otьci*, nom. pl. *otьci*, acc. pl. *otьcę*, instr. pl. *otьci*, loc. pl. *otьcixъ*); consequently, hypothesis I, as well as hypothesis Ia, must be rejected.

8. HYPOTHESIS II: The change $k > č$ preceded the change $k > c$ (or, to be precise, $k > c'$) resulting from the progressive palatalization.

9. SPECIAL HYPOTHESIS IIA: The change $k > č$, preceding the shift $k > c$ (c'), occurred before every front vowel, regardless of its origin. If we were to totally ignore the relative chronology of the emergence of secondary front vowels (so-called $ě_2$, $-i_2$) with respect to the effect of the palatalization $k > č$, we would, in all likelihood, be unable to explain the nominative plural form *otьci*. Such would be the case at any rate if we assume, with the majority of specialists, that the second regressive palatalization took place earlier than, or, rather, began to operate earlier than, the progressive palatalization. When it comes to accounting for the remaining forms with a front vowel (i.e., the instr. and loc. sg. *otьcemь*, *otьci*; dat.-instr. dual *otьcema*; and the gen., dat., acc., instr., loc. pl. *otьcь*, *otьcemь*, *otьcę*, *otьci*, *otьcixъ*), we have to assume various analogical levelings patterned on the proportions obtaining between hard-stem (*-o*) and soft-stem (*-jo*) desinences. In other words, we are concerned here not with instances of phonological change, but rather with morphological generalizations.[26] Only if we were to accept the view advocated by Knutsson, Ekblom, Mareš (and some others) that the progressive palatalization actually took place earlier than the second regressive palatalization, would it presumably be possible to interpret the nominative plural form as resulting from the Baudouin palatalization: *at(t)ikoi > *otьc'oi > otьci*. However, such an order of shifts appears less likely.

10. SPECIAL HYPOTHESIS IIB: Consequently, it is more reasonable to assume that the change $k > č$ occurred prior not only to the shift $k > c$ (under the conditions of the progressive palatalization), but also to the rise of the secondary front vowels $ě_2$, $-i_2$, resulting from a monophthongization of former diphthongs. For an explanation of most forms with a following (analogical) front vowel, see *sub* 9, above.

[26]   Cf., for example, G. Y. Shevelov, *A Prehistory of Slavic*, 348-349.

It should be pointed out that the postulates just quoted (1-10) by no means claim to be either exhaustive or otherwise definitive. Rather, they were adduced here merely for the purpose of illustrating the great complexity of linguistic factors calling for an explanation before we can even begin to formulate and assign synchronic phonological rules to generate correct forms, attested or potential as the case may be, in this long extinct and only fragmentarily recorded literary language. However, the elucidation of these complex factors involves, as we have tried to demonstrate, accounting also for certain historical (diachronic) data which cannot be obtained merely by relying on the method of internal reconstruction, that is to say, in this case by resorting only to synchronic data of Old Church Slavic. Even so, in the above-formulated postulates we have endeavored to limit the number of diachronic considerations to an absolute minimum.

Whereas the method of merely applying a number of ordered generative rules to synchronic data of Old Church Slavic presents great difficulty in an attempt to establish the relative chronology between the first regressive and the progressive (Baudouin) palatalizations of velars in Common Slavic, this method is even less satisfactory when it comes to establishing the highly controversial relative chronology of the progressive and the second regressive palatalizations, respectively, i.e., processes yielding basically identical results, *viz.*, dental affricates and fricatives (except for the alveolar *š* in West Slavic). One of the main reasons for the seemingly insurmountable difficulties in establishing a relative chronology between these two processes appears to be the fact that they most probably partly overlapped in time.[27]

[27] Cf. G.Y. Shevelov, *A Prehistory of Slavic*, 351-354 and A. Vaillant, *Grammaire comparée des langues slaves* I (Lyon–Paris, 1950), 49-55. In the practice of classroom teaching it may therefore be advisable to distinguish only between two basic palatalizations of velars in Common Slavic: a first (type $k > č$) and a second (type $k > c$), specifying, to the extent known, the two sets of conditions under which the second palatalization would occur (*viz.*, (1) before secondary front vowels, and (2) after certain, originally high or diffuse, front vowels; notice, however, that the second condition is not exhaustively formulated, additional details being controversial.) For a brief discussion of what seems to be non-occurrence of the second palatalization even under the first

V.J. Zeps, in a recent paper on the palatalizations of velars as evidenced by Old Church Slavic, has challenged the claim that any particular parallelism can be ascertained between sets of ordered synchronic and diachronic rules.[28] Commencing his discussion with the statement, "it is a commonplace that morphophonemics to some degree mirrors history, i.e. that historical changes survive as morphophonemic alternations", he proceeds to demonstrate, on the basis of the two regressive palatalizations reflected in Old Church Slavic, that the undisputed relative chronology of these two historical processes and the body of ordered generative rules devised to account for both alternations (k, g, x / $č$, $ž$, $š$, as well as k, g, x / c, dz, s) in a unified fashion, cannot be conceived as matching each other in a one-to-one relationship. Thus, the historical relative chronology of these two palatalizations can be summarized and illustrated as follows:

1. Proto-Slavic Input: *vlьke,[29] *koina
2. First Palatalization: vlьče, *koina
3. Monophthongization: vlьče, *kěna
4. Second Palatalization: vlьče, cěna

On the other hand, at least one of the possible ways of conceiving the internal order of rules to account for the phonetic realization underlying the abstract input forms is the following:

1. Monophthongization ($oi > ě$)

---

condition, see section 5 (numbered 10) of my article, "Zur Problematik...", to appear in *ZfslPh*, referred to in fn. 1.

[28] Cf. V.J. Zeps, "A Synchronic and Diachronic Order of Rules: Mutations of Velars in Old Church Slavonic", in *Approaches in Linguistic Methodology*, I. Rauch, and C.T. Scott (eds.), (Madison–Milwaukee–London, 1967), 145-151.

[29] The form *vlьke quoted by Zeps (*op. cit.*, 146) does not, of course, correspond to any historical reality since we rather must assume an actual form *vъlke for the early Proto-Slavic period; cf. OR vъlkъ, CSR volk, PO wilk. Zeps' form should therefore be considered a simplified abstraction to illustrate only the sound change under discussion. Further, the form vlьče, given for Old Church Slavic, while representing a possible spelling, is not the most usual one. More frequently, the syllabic liquid is rendered lъ, regardless of its origin.

2. Second palatalization (k, g, $x > c$, dz, s)
3. First palatalization (k, g, $x > č$, $ž$, $š$)[30]

To be sure, Zeps then offers a number of reasonable alternatives, either reshaping the order of his rules so as to parallel the presumed historical order or unifying the two crucial (palatalization) rules into one, with its components, however, to be considered in a 'non-historical' order.[31] As a result, he suggests not only "the strong possibility that the synchronic and diachronic order of rules can disagree", but also questions "the credibility of internal reconstruction, especially if it involves the type of details and time depth in reconstructions of Proto-IE from IE, and the like". The major new contribution to diachronic linguistics that Zeps, along with others, expects of formal (i.e., generative) grammar is, in addition to lending more rigor and precision to its traditional findings, the subsequent writing of histories of grammars (sets of rules), rather than merely historical descriptions of data reconstructable or attested at various stages in linguistic evolution.

By contrast, N. Chomsky and M. Halle, in their detailed and more comprehensive treatment of Slavic palatalizations (including also the dental — t, d, s, z — palatalizations before a nonback and high glide — j, in their notation /y/ — and, like Zeps, excluding from consideration the progressive, so-called Baudouin palatalization), seem to arrive at a different order of rules which indeed would parallel the well-established relative chronology of the two regressive velar palatalizations.[32] The dating of the dental palatalization (leading partly to the same results as the first velar palatalization) and the order of rules accounting for the various reflexes of tj, dj, sj, zj in South, East and West Slavic, respectively, are of a different kind and will be discussed here only peripherally.

---

[30] Cf. Zeps, *op. cit.*, 149. Zeps' set of processes is actually more elaborate, containing six different rules. The ones cited above correspond to his rules 2, 3, and 4, respectively; rules 1, 5, and 6, though by no means dispensable, can be disregarded in this context.

[31] Cf. Zeps, *op. cit.*, 150.

[32] Cf. N. Chomsky and M. Halle, *The Sound Pattern of English* (New York, 1968), 420-430; in particular, see 423-426 for the velar palatalizations, 428-430 for the dental palatalizations.

Omitting all sophisticated, if partly arguable, detail, we note that the rules accounting for the first and second palatalizations of velars in Slavic are given by Chomsky and Halle in just this order, i.e., the rule yielding the results of the first palatalization comes first (rule 26), and the rule for the second palatalization only subsequently (rule 34 for South and East Slavic, and rule 39 for West Slavic). The rules accounting for the dental palatalization follow that for the second palatalization in South and East Slavic, respectively (rule 44 and rule 42), while in West Slavic the dental palatalization rule is inserted between the rules of the two velar palatalizations (rule 45).[33] Notice, finally, as pointed out by the two authors, "that if the Second Palatalization were not restricted to non-strident consonants, it would affect the segments produced by the First Palatalization Rule, turning these, as well as the remaining velars, into strident dentals. If this were actually the desired results, there would then be no need for the First Palatalization Rule, since the output of the grammar would be the same whether or not it included this rule. These considerations are of more than abstract interest since the well-known *mazurzenie* phenomenon of Polish (and, one may add, the *cokan'e* of dialectal Russian, the so-called *cakavism* of some northwestern dialects of Serbo-Croatian, as well as related phenomena in Ukrainian dialects, Slovene, Sorbian, and Polabian, *H. B.*) is precisely of this type and would be formally characterized in the manner just outlined."[34]

In concluding these brief remarks regarding the claimed parallelism between relative chronology of diachronic phonological changes and a well-defined order in the application of synchronic generative rules of the phonological component (or, to be exact, at the level which traditionally has been referred to as morphophonemics[35]), it is important, I believe, to voice a word of warning as regards this parallelism. Although M. Halle in particular has

---

[33] Cf. the summary, *Sound Pattern*, 430, chart 46.
[34] Cf. *Sound Pattern*, 426, fn. 14.
[35] For a brief discussion of the less well-understood differences between systematic phonemics (in generative grammar) and traditional morphophonemics, see P.M. Postal, *Aspects of Phonological Theory* (New York, 1968), xii, fn. 9.

claimed such a parallelism (which, no doubt, can frequently be ascertained) to be non-accidental in character, serious reservations remain as to this non-accidental, or rather motivated, nature of it. Whatever the case, this parallelism should not be cited as a major factor to justify the specific ordering of generative phonological rules. The order of such rules must rather be determined by the criteria of economy and maximal simplicity, while still meeting the adequacy requirement of linguistic description.[36]

3. Next, let us consider how far back we can trace linguistic evolution, having recourse only to the method of internal reconstruction. Here, in particular, we must address ourselves to the following question: If we were to apply only the method of internal reconstruction to synchronic data of Late Common Slavic, say, of the 7th-9th cc.,[37] and if we were to take as our point of departure this Late Common Slavic stage (reconstructed by means of the comparative method on the basis of the various historically attested Slavic languages, especially in their oldest recorded state), would it be possible — omitting, to be sure, many details — to arrive at the earliest, i.e., initial, phase of Proto-Slavic or, in other words, at the point of the emergence from Common Balto-Slavic of a language which could be considered specifically Slavic? As far as we know, no one has yet undertaken a coherent and systematic attempt towards solving this difficult problem.[38] (It is, of course,

---

[36] Cf., in particular, M. Halle's article, "On the Role of Simplicity in Linguistic Description", quoted above (fn. 15).

[37] For a discussion of the problem of defining the upper time limit of Common Slavic, see H. Birnbaum, "The Dialects of Common Slavic", *Ancient Indo-European Dialects*, 153-197, esp. 153-156; *Id.*, "On Some Problems of Common Slavic Dialectology", *IJSLP* IX (1965), 1-19, esp. 1-3; and, in particular, now also my forthcoming article, "Zur Problematik...", *ZfslPh*, esp. section 4 (numbered 6 and 7).

[38] This contention therefore does not pertain to the many sporadic and unsystematic attempts (as scattered throughout textbooks, monographs, and various articles and contributions) in applying the method of internal reconstruction to recreate certain partial evolutions which had occurred in the Common Slavic period. A consistent concept of a systematic and more comprehensive reconstruction of the changes which the phonological and morphological components (or the 'linguistic model') of Common Slavic had undergone

an entirely different matter that the initial phase of Proto-Slavic can be recovered to some extent by comparing the data of Late Common Slavic — itself reconstructed by comparison of individual Slavic languages — with linguistic facts from without the Slavic group, that is to say, in particular with data of the closely related Baltic languages.)[39]

While it seems possible, at least theoretically, to reconstruct to some extent the earlier periods of Common Slavic on internal evidence from Late Common Slavic, the same can be said only with great reservations about the application of this method to Baltic material. Here, internal reconstruction encounters serious methodological difficulties. The main reason for the discrepancy in the potential reconstruction of the common predecessors of the Slavic and Baltic languages, respectively, is, naturally, the very fact that the disintegration of the Slavic linguistic community coincides roughly with the appearance of attested Slavic writing, so that one cannot really speak of any significant time gap between the final period of Common Slavic and the beginning of Old Church Slavic literacy while, in contrast, the written tradition of the Baltic languages does not reach as far back in time. Of the latter group only three are, as we know, attested: Old Prussian, representing the West Baltic group; and Lithuanian and Latvian, representing the

---

from its very inception (i.e., as of its emergence from Balto-Slavic) to Late Common Slavic, moving retrogressively through time, was outlined and illustrated by the Soviet linguists V.V. Ivanov and V.N. Toporov in an insightful paper presented at the Fourth International Congress of Slavists (Moscow, 1958), "O postanovke voprosa...", *Issledovanija...*, 273-305 (for full reference, see fn. 19). Cf. further the article by V.N. Toporov, "Nekotorye soobraženija otnositel'no izučenija istorii praslavjanskogo jazyka", *Slavjanskoe jazykoznanie. Sbornik statej* (Moscow, 1959), 3-27, (with additional references, particularly to some work by N.S. Trubeckoj); cf. also the writings by Ivanov and Toporov cited in fn. 3, above.

[39] This is the approach taken, for example, by P. Arumaa in his *Urslavische Grammatik*; cf. esp. also his programmatic statement, *op. cit.*, 6: "Der Verfasser hat...in erster Linie versucht, den frühesten uns erreichbaren Übergang vom Indogermanischen zum Urslavischen lautlich zu fixieren, d.h. die älteste und möglichst sichere Unterlage zur Rekonstruktion des Urslavischen aufzuzeigen." For a general appraisal of this manual, see my review in *IJSLP* X (1966), 165-178.

East Baltic group. The oldest Baltic text, the so-called *Elbing Vocabulary* is usually thought to date from ca. 1400. The earliest known Lithuanian text, the so-called *Dzukovian Prayers*, are believed to have been written around 1515; and the first Latvian texts, two catechisms and a song book, appear only in the 80's of the 16th century.[40] Many centuries, and perhaps as much as one and a half millenia, must have elapsed between the disintegration of the Baltic linguistic unity (if indeed we can assume that such a relatively homogeneous unity actually ever existed) and the beginnings of Baltic writing. Consequently, the differences between the individual Baltic languages, even in their oldest known form, are much more pronounced than the dissimilarities among the Slavic languages. This close relationship holding among these latter languages is especially apparent, if we go beyond their present form and compare their earliest attested stages when the differences separating them were even less significant. The kind of dialectal differentiation found in Baltic, on the other hand, occasionally seems to reflect discrepancies which already existed in Late Common Indo-European. A few examples can illustrate this claim.

Thus, as shown by J. Endzelīns, the change $s > š$ occurred in Lithuanian basically only in the position after r and k while the same change appears, at least superficially, to be altogether unknown in Old Prussian and Latvian. Another possible interpretation would suggest that this sound shift did indeed take place throughout the entire Baltic linguistic area, but is no longer discernible in either Old Prussian owing to its awkward orthography patterned on that of Middle Low German, or in Latvian, because of the subsequent merging of s and $š$ (the present Latvian $š$ is of different origin). On the other hand, the corresponding changes $s > š$ and $s > x$, respectively, encompassed both the entire Indo-

---

[40] For a discussion of the possibility of even assuming an actual overlap between Late Common Slavic and early attested Slavic, see, in particular, section 4 (numbered 6 and 7) of my paper "Zur Problematik...", to appear in *ZfslPh*. For details on the recently discovered *Dzukovian Prayers*, extending the attested history of Lithuanian by a few decades, see A. Senn, *Handbuch der litauischen Sprache*, I: *Grammatik* (Heidelberg, 1966), 50-51, 53-54, and 56. (This Old Lithuanian text was first published in 1964.)

Iranian and Slavic territories, occurring in the environment after *i, u, r, k* and its allophones (some negligible deviations being disregarded here).[41] Further, an epenthetic *-t-* was inserted in the consonantal cluster *sr* (> *str*), not only throughout Slavic and Germanic (cf. OCS *struja, ostrovъ*; ModGerm *Strom*, ONorse *straumr*, etc.), but also in the Balkan Indo-European languages Thracian and Illyrian (cf. such toponyms as Illyr *Stravianae* or *Strevintia* and the Thracian hydronym Στρύμων). In Baltic, on the other hand, this phenomenon seems to be largely restricted to Old Prussian (cf. the geographical names *Strewe, Nastrayn, Stromyke, Strowange*) and Latvian (cf., for example, *stràva*), while in Lithuanian it is confined primarily to some of the dialects (cf., for example, CSLith *sráigė* vs. dial. Lith *stráigė*; CSLith *sraujà* vs. dial. Lith *Straujà*, a river name; CSLith *srově* vs. dial. Lith *strově*, and the like). Another example, this time from morphology, is the genitive singular ending of the *o*-stems in Old Prussian (type *deiwas*), usually derived from the Indo-European desinence *-o-so* (reflected also in Germanic). The other Baltic languages, Lithuanian and Latvian, show here endings corresponding to their Slavic counterparts (Lith *diẽvo, vilko*; Latv *tẽva*; OCS *vlъka*), which can be traced back to a Balto-Slavic form *-ā*, apparently mirroring the old ablative desinence of the *o*-stems, *viz.* *-ōd* (cf. the Early Latin and Oscan residues of an ablative in *-ōd*).[42] Moreover, one could say that some of the differences found among Lithuanian dialects are fundamentally more far-reaching than the dissimilarities among individual Slavic languages, including even those which form the basis of the traditional classification into East, West, and South Slavic, respectively (a classification which remains valid also in the light of modern areal linguistics[43]). Therefore, in those relatively

[41] For a new intriguing interpretation of the change under discussion, in terms of distinctive features, and using the notion of markedness assimilation, see H. Andersen, "IE *s after *i, u, r, k* in Baltic and Slavic", *Acta Linguistica Hafniensia*. XI: 2 (1968), 171-190.
[42] For some more details, see C. Watkins, *Ancient Indo-European Dialects*, 37-39 (in his contribution "Italo-Celtic Revisited").
[43] Cf. H. Birnbaum, *Ancient Indo-European Dialects*, 194-197 (in my contribution "The Dialects of Common Slavic"); *Id., IJSLP* IX (1965), 15-19.

few instances where we are able to recover certain fragments of an earlier Baltic linguistic structure by means of internal reconstruction, we can at least, as a rule, reach much more remote times than is possible in the reconstruction of previous periods of Common Slavic. On the other hand, as regards the last phase of Baltic unity there can be no doubt that, even taking into consideration the absence of early records, this end phase, as indicated by absolute chronology, must have preceded the equivalent Common Slavic phase by many centuries. It may therefore be legitimate to see in the generally recognized archaic character of the Baltic languages, in particular Old Prussian and Lithuanian, a kind of projection of the situation prevailing in Proto-Baltic.[44] If this is in fact the case, the conclusion reached by V. V. Ivanov and V. N. Toporov founded on both theoretical considerations and the contemplation of concrete linguistic data (viewed, to be sure, in the framework of their overall structures) seems indeed quite logical. According to these Soviet linguists "the model, established for Slavic" must be considered "the result of a transformation of the model established for the earliest Baltic state", whereas a reverse interpretation, i.e., a derivation of the Proto-Baltic from early Proto-Slavic, does not seem conceivable.[45] In this context it should perhaps be mentioned that another Baltologist, approaching the problem from entirely different (and, in my view, less convincing) premises, reached an analogical conclusion regarding the earliest Balto-Slavic linguistic relations.[46]

The basic conclusion reached by Ivanov and Toporov that the Proto-Slavic linguistic model (i.e., roughly speaking, the phonemic and morphemic structure of Early Common Slavic) can be derived from the more archaic model of Proto-Baltic, while denying the possibility of a reverse process, also sheds some new light on the

[44] Cf. V. V. Ivanov and V. N. Toporov, *Issledovanija...*, 276.
[45] See *ibid.*, 303 with detailed argumentation, 303-304.
[46] Cf. A. Senn, "The Relationships of Baltic and Slavic", *Ancient Indo-European Dialects*, 139-151, esp. 139 (polemizing with O. Szemerényi). For some criticism of Senn's position, see my forthcoming paper, "Four Approaches to Balto-Slavic", contributed to the Festschrift for Chr. S. Stang, *Donum Balticum*.

above-discussed question of a parallelism between internal reconstruction as applied to the phonological component (leading to the
establishment of relative chronologies) and the order of synchronic
generative rules at the morphophonemic ('systematic phonemic')
level. In this context it ought to be mentioned that the order of
applying synchronic phonological rules does not relate so much to
the method of internal reconstruction itself, but points up the analogy with relative chronology established, to be sure, primarily by
means of this very method. In other words, whenever we have to
resort also to the comparative method for the establishment of
relative chronologies (as is frequently the case), this by no means
precludes the analogy between relative chronology and the order
of synchronic rules required for the rewriting of the morphophonemics of a given language to produce the desired evolutionary
state, i.e., usually its contemporary form. Thus, for example, as
previously mentioned, T. M. Lightner has attempted to formulate
a set of rules by means of which a considerable number of underlying morphemes generally resembling Proto-Slavic could be re-
written so as to yield their Contemporary Standard Polish equivalents.[47] In so doing, all changes which occurred in the course of
the development of Common Slavic and Polish, respectively, can,
in principle at least, be recovered by means of the method of
internal reconstruction, while the processes characteristic of the
development from Late Common Slavic to Proto-Polish (passing

[47]   Cf. T. M. Lightner, "Preliminary Remarks on the Morphophonemic Component of Polish", (see further fn. 15, above). It should be pointed out, however, that although the input forms assumed by Lightner have a largely Proto-
Slavic appearance (the equivalent Contemporary Standard Polish being the
output forms), not all of them fully correspond to the forms which can be
reconstructed on the basis of a comparison with other Indo-European languages.
Thus, for instance, Lightner posits input forms ending in -os (+ oŝ, in his
notation) for the genitive plural (miąs < mENŝ + oŝ, rąk < rONk + oŝ)
where the evidence suggested by the comparative method shows that we have
to reconstruct original forms in *-ōm; cf. QPR 71 (1963), 226 (examples 2 and
5). Further, it should be remembered that the order of synchronic rules,
determined by the principle of simplicity and economy, though frequently
matching relative chronology as established by internal or comparative reconstruction, or even as suggested by the attested data of linguistic evolution,
is far from always in accordance with the facts of chronology.

through the stages of dialectal Common Slavic, Common West Slavic, and Northwest Slavic or Lekhitic, in this order) can be established only with the aid of the comparative method as well.[48] If, therefore, we are to accept as well-founded the Soviet linguists' conclusion regarding the derivability of the Proto-Slavic model from an Early Common Baltic model, we would have to assume that rewrite rules analogical to those formulated by Lightner for the development from Proto-Slavic through Modern Polish could be supplemented by a set of additional rules enabling us to derive the Proto-Slavic forms from (or, put differently, trace them back to) the Proto-Baltic input forms.

Just as the relative chronology of diachronic data and the order of phonological rules applied to synchronic data show certain correspondences (though perhaps not really a considerable parallelism), so the method of projected prediction, to the extent it can be applied to the data of one particular language at a specific stage in its development, may be considered a corollary to the method of internal reconstruction. For it can be shown that the application of a set of phonological rules to synchronic linguistic data implies the employment of a method of prediction since the output of these rules is predictable, in theory at least, on the strength of the properly formulated rules. In this context we are, for the time being, not so much concerned with the practical question whether it is indeed possible to formulate such morphophonemic rules which would permit us to predict, more or less completely and systematically, for example, a set of Proto-Slavic forms, using as input only their reconstructed Proto-Baltic equivalents and relying on our theoreti-

---

[48] For details regarding the complicated course of dialectal development in the Late Common Slavic period, see H. Birnbaum, "The Dialects of Common Slavic", *Ancient Indo-European Dialects*, 153-197, with references to relevant literature (159-160 and *passim*); and *Id.*, "On Some Problems of Common Slavic Dialectology", *IJSLP* IX (1965), 1-19. For some remarks critical of my interpretation of the main problems of Common Slavic dialectology, see E. Weiher, "Urslavisch-Gemeinslavisch-Dialekte des Gemeinslavischen (?)", [sic!] *Anzeiger für slavische Philologie* II (1967), 82-100. For a rejoinder to his critique, see the relevant comments in my article, "Zur Problematik ...", *ZfslPh* (to appear).

cal assumptions as to the form of the Proto-Slavic items which would constitute the output of this reshaping process; rather, at this point, we are primarily interested in the purely theoretical aspects of this problem.[49]

Only if we go beyond the narrow framework of specifically internal reconstruction and employ methods of reconstruction in general to recover past linguistic stages not immediately accessible through preserved records, i.e., methods not only of internal, but also of comparative and external reconstruction (cf. above), can we also extend the analogy between the methods of reconstruction (in their broadest sense) and the methods of prediction in linguistics. For if it is true that genetic linguistics, dealing primarily with problems of relationships between languages and language families (including protolanguages from which these families can be derived), is the primary domain where various methods of reconstruction can be applied, then it is equally valid that different devices elaborated for the purpose of predicting future developments (whether this future is conceived in absolute terms or relatively, as viewed from the vantage point of some past period) find their application principally in the field of typological linguistics and, particularly, within one of its sub-spheres. I have in mind the sub-discipline which, by supplementing the major typological criteria with some secondary areal considerations, examines not so much the manifestations of linguistic divergence as it does the phenomena of linguistic integration and convergence of languages within clearly defined geographical areas where these languages, regardless of any prior affinity, merge into new groupings often referred to as

---

[49]   For some more thoughts on the correlation obtaining between the methods of reconstruction and prediction, see my paper, "On Reconstruction and Prediction: Two Correlates in Genetic and Typological Linguistics", *Folia Linguistica* II (1969), 1-17, also reprinted above, pp. 71-91; in particular, for its relevance to Balto-Slavic data, see also my paper, "On the Reconstruction and Predictability of Linguistic Models: Balto-Slavic Revisited", *Scando-Slavica* XIII (1967), 105-114; cf. now further also the paper by E. Pulgram, "Trends and Prediction", *To Honor Roman Jakobson* II (The Hague-Paris, 1967), 1634-1649, adducing primarily linguistic data of a different nature and taking a somewhat different approach.

Sprachbünde.[50] Thus, for example, the method of predicting future language developments promises to yield interesting results in the field of Balkan linguistics where, in recent years, some scholars have assumed the existence of an underlying abstract metalinguistic model toward which, apparently, most, if not all, of the typical Balkan languages (i.e., the members of the Balkan linguistic convergence area) are tending.[51]

In the light of the preceding discussion then, new significance is brought to R. Jakobson's remarks regarding typological and genetic linguistics in his memorable report to the 8th International Congress of Linguists, when he quoted J. H. Greenberg's words that "the typology of languages adds to our predictive power", and recalled F. Schlegel's dictum that the historian is as a prophet predicting backward — an image applicable both to diachronic linguistics as

---

[50] Several English equivalents for German *Sprachbund*, Russian *jazykovoj sojuz*, French *union linguistique*, etc. have been proposed and are currently in use. The term 'convergence area', coined by the late U. Weinreich (*Word* XIV [1958], 379), focusing on the geographical setting, rather than on the linguistic phenomena *per se*, seems perhaps most satisfactory.

[51] The typical Balkan languages include, as is known, Romanian (with two of its isolated dialects in the Balkans, Arumanian and Meglenitic), Albanian, Modern Greek, Bulgarian, Macedonian, as well as certain southeast dialects of Serbian, especially the transitional, Torlak dialect group. For recent work in Balkan linguistics, along the lines indicated above, see T. V. Civ'jan, *Imja suščestvitel'noe v balkanskix jazykax. K strukturnotipologičeskoj xarakteristike balkanskogo jazykovogo sojuza* (Moscow, 1965); cf. esp. her theoretical remarks, 15-16, 22, and 183-189 and 191-192. See also my review of Civ'jan's book, *Zeitschrift für Balkanologie* IV (1966), 175-181; cf. further my articles "Balkanslavisch und Südslavisch: Zur Reichweite der Balkanismen im südslavischen Sprachraum", *ZfB* III (1965), 12-63; "Slavjanskie jazyki na Balkanax i ponjatie tak nazyvaemyx jazykovyx sojuzov", *Glossa* II (1968), 10-92; "On Typology, Affinity and Balkan Linguistics", *Zbornik za filologiju i lingvistiku* IX (1966), 17-30, where, among other things, it is suggested that only genetic and typological characteristics can be used as basic equal criteria for the classification of languages, while areal criteria can never have more than secondary significance, supplementing the fundamental, genetic and/or typological classificatory criteria. For a revision of this view, subordinating the criteria of genetic linguistics to those of typological linguistics, and introducing the notion of stratified deep structure, see my paper, "Deep Structure and Typological Linguistics", included in this volume (pp. 9-70). For a tentative application of a generative approach to Balkan linguistics, see also K. Kazazis, "On a Generative Grammar of the Balkan Languages", *Foundations of Language* III (1967), 117-123.

a whole, in contrast to language typology, and to methods of re-construction in particular, as opposed to methods of prediction in linguistics.[52]

---

[52] Cf. R. Jakobson, "Typological Studies and Their Contribution to Historical Comparative Linguistics", *Proceedings of the Eighth International Congress of Linguists* (Oslo, 1958), 17-25, esp. 23 (reprinted also in his *Selected Writings* I [The Hague, 1962], 523-530, esp. 528); cf. also the pertinent comments by V.V. Ivanov, published in the *Proceedings*, 25-27.

BIBLIOGRAPHY

Afendras, E. A., *The Balkans as a Linguistic Area: A Study in Phonological Convergence* (The Johns Hopkins University, 1968) (Photomechanic reproduction of unpublished doctoral dissertation).

Allen, W. S., "Relationship in Comparative Linguistics", in: *Transactions of the Philological Society* (London, 1953), 52-108.

Ambrazas, V., "Absoliutinis naudininkas XVI-XVIIa. lietuvių kalbos paminkluose", in: *Lietuvių kalbotyros klausimai* V (Vilnius, 1962), 56-80.

American Contributions to the Fifth International Congress of Slavists, I: *Linguistic Contributions* (The Hague, 1963).

American Contributions to the Sixth International Congress of Slavists, I: *Linguistic Contributions*, H. Kučera, ed. (The Hague-Paris, 1968).

Ancient Indo-European Dialects. Proceedings of the Conference on Indo-European Linguistics at UCLA, April 25-27, 1963, H. Birnbaum and J. Puhvel, eds. (Berkeley-Los Angeles, 1966).

Andersen, H., "IE *s after *i, u, r, k* in Baltic and Slavic", *Acta Linguistica Hafniensia* XI:2 (1968), 171-190.

——, "The Dative of Subordination in Baltic and Slavic", in: *Baltic Linguistics*, T. F. Magner, W. R. Schmalstieg, eds. (University Park and London, 1970), 1-9.

Anttila, R., "The Relation Between Internal Reconstruction and the Comparative Method", *Ural-Altaische Jahrbücher* XL (1968), 159-173.

Apresjan, Ju. D., *Èksperimental'noe issledovanie semantiki russkogo glagola* (Moscow, 1967).

Arumaa, P., *Urslavische Grammatik*, I (Heidelberg, 1964).

Bach, E., R.T. Harms, eds., see *Universals in Linguistic Theory*.

Bar-Hillel, Y., "Universal Semantics and Philosophy of Language: Quandaries and Prospects", in: *Substance and Structure of Language*, 1-21.

Becker, H., *Der Sprachbund* (Berlin-Leipzig, 1948).

Beiträge zur Sprachwissenschaft, Volkskunde und Literaturforschung. W. Steinitz zum 60. Geburtstag am 28. Februar 1965 dargebracht, A. V. Isačenko *et al.*, eds. (Berlin, 1965).

[Birnbaum, G. =] Birnbaum, H., "Obščeslavjanskoe nasledie i inojazyčnye obrazcy v strukturnyx raznovidnostjax staroslavjanskogo predloženija", in: *American Contributions to the Sixth International Congress of Slavists*, I, 29-63.

Birnbaum, H., "Balkanslavisch und Südslavisch: Zur Reichweite der Balkanismen im südslavischen Sprachraum", *ZfBalk* III (1965), 12-63.

——, "Four Approaches to Balto-Slavic", in: *Donum Balticum* (Festschrift for Chr. S. Stang; forthcoming).

——, "On Deep Structure and Loan Syntax in Slavic", in: *Studies in Slavic Linguistics and Poetics in Honor of Boris O. Unbegaun*, R. Magidoff, G. Y. Shevelov, J. S. G. Simmons, K. Taranovski, J. E. Allen III, eds. (New York, 1968), 21-31.

——, "On Reconstruction and Prediction: Two Correlates of Diachrony in Genetic and Typological Linguistics", *FL* II (1969), 1-17 (reprinted in this volume, pp. 71-91).

——, "On Some Problems of Common Slavic Dialectology", *IJSLP* IX (1965), 1-19.

——, "On the Reconstruction and Predictability of Linguistic Models: Balto-Slavic Revisited", *ScSl* XIII (1967), 105-114.

——, "On Typology, Affinity, and Balkan Linguistics", *Zbornik za filologiju i lingvistiku* IX (1966), 17-30.

——, "Predication and the Russian Infinitive", in: *To Honor Roman Jakobson*, I (The Hague, 1967), 271-294.

——, "Rekonstrukcja wewnętrzna, kolejność synchronicznych reguł gramatyki syntetycznej i zagadnienie najdawniejszych stosunków między językami bałtyckimi a słowiańskimi", *IJSLP* XI (1968), 1-24 (revised English version reprinted in this volume, pp. 92-122).

——, [Review of] P. Arumaa, *Urslavische Grammatik*, I, *IJSLP* X (1966), 165-178.

——, [Review of] T. V. Civ'jan, *Imja suščestvitel'noe v balkanskix jazykax. K strukturno-tipologičeskoj xarakteristike balkanskogo jazykovogo sojuza*, *ZfBalk* IV (1966), 173-181.

——, [Review of] T. Milewski, *Językoznawstwo*, *Lg* XLIII (1967), 751-757.

——, *Studies on Predication in Russian*, II: *On the Predicative Use of the Russian Infinitive* (= Memorandum RM-4477-PR, The RAND Corporation) (Santa Monica, Cal., 1965).

——, "The Dialects of Common Slavic", in: *Ancient Indo-European Dialects*, 153-197.

——, *Untersuchungen zu den Zukunftsumschreibungen mit dem Infinitiv im Altkirchenslavischen. Ein Beitrag zur historischen Verbalsyntax des Slavischen* (Stockholm, 1958).

——, "Zur Problematik der zeitlichen Abgrenzung des Urslavischen (Über die Relativität der Begriffe Baltoslavisch/Frühurslavisch bzw. Spätgemeinslavischer Dialekt/Ureinzelslavine)", *ZfslPh* XXXV (1970) (forthcoming).

——, and J. Puhvel, eds., see *Ancient Indo-European Dialects*.

[Birnbaum, X. =] Birnbaum, H., "Slavjanskie jazyki na Balkanax i ponjatie tak nazyvaemyx jazykovyx sojuzov", *Glossa* II (1968), 70-92.

Blanár, V., "Über strukturelle Übereinstimmungen im Wortschatz der Balkansprachen", in: *Recueil linguistique de Bratislava*, II (Bratislava, 1968), 80-97.

Borkovskij, V. I., ed., see *Sravnitel'no-istoričeskij sintaksis vostočnoslavjanskix jazykov*.

Borkovskij, V. I. and P. S. Kuznecov, *Istoričeskaja grammatika russkogo jazyka*, 2nd ed. (Moscow, 1965).

BSL = *Bulletin de la Société de linguistique de Paris.*
Chafe, W. L., *Explorations in the Theory of Language* (forthcoming).
——, "Internal Reconstruction in Seneca", *Lg* XXXV (1959), 477-495.
——, "Language as Symbolization", *Lg* XLIII (1967), 57-91.
Chomsky, N., *Aspects of the Theory of Syntax* (Cambridge, Mass., 1965).
——, *Cartesian Linguistics* (New York, 1966).
——, *Current Issues in Linguistic Theory* (The Hague, 1964).
——, "Deep Structure, Surface Structure, and Semantic Interpretation" (forthcoming, to appear in the Festschrift for S. Hattori).
——, *Syntactic Structures*, 3rd printing (The Hague, 1963).
——, "The Formal Nature of Language" = Appendix A, in: E. H. Lenneberg, *Biological Foundations of Language* (New York, 1967), 397-442.
——, *Topics in the Theory of Generative Grammar* (The Hague, 1966) (appeared simultaneously also in: *Current Trends*, III, 1-60).
——, and M. Halle, *The Sound Pattern of English* (New York, 1968).
Civ'jan, T. V., *Imja suščestvitel'noe v balkanskix jazykax. K strukturno-tipologičeskoj xarakteristike balkanskogo jazykovogo sojuza* (Moscow, 1965).
——, "Opyt opisanija form novogrečeskogo suščestvitel'nogo metodom analiza i sinteza", *VJa* 1963: 6, 57-68.
Current Trends, III = *Current Trends in Linguistics*, T. A. Sebeok, ed., III: *Theoretical Foundations* (The Hague, 1966).
Cyxun, G. A., *Sintaksis mestoimennyx klitik v južnoslavjanskix jazykax* (*Balkanoslavjanskaja model'*) (Minsk, 1968).
Dahl, Ö., *Topic and Comment: A Study in Russian and General Transformational Grammar* (Gothenburg, 1969).
Ebeling, C. L., "Questions of Relative Chronology in Common Slavic and Russian Phonology", in: *Dutch Contributions to the Fifth International Congress of Slavicists* (The Hague, 1963), 27-42.
Ekblom, R., *Die frühe dorsale Palatalisierung im Slavischen* (Uppsala, 1951).
Ellis, J., *Towards a General Comparative Linguistics* (The Hague, 1966).
[Endzelin, J. =] Endzelīns, J., *Lettische Grammatik* (Riga, 1922).
Endzelīns, J., *Latviešu valodas gramatika* (Riga, 1951).
Enkvist, N. E., "Tre modeller för ljudhistorisk forskning" = *Societas Scientiarum Fennica*, XLIV, B, 4 (Helsinki, 1966).
Fillmore, C. J., "The Case for Case", in: *Universals in Linguistic Theory*, 1-88.
FL = *Folia Linguistica.*
Fodor, I., *The Rate of Linguistic Change: Limits of the Application of Mathematical Methods in Linguistics* (The Hague, 1965).
Fodor, J. A., J. J. Katz, eds., see *The Structure of Language.*
Fokos-Fuchs, D. R., *Rolle der Syntax in der Frage nach der Sprachverwandtschaft mit besonderer Rücksicht auf das Problem der ural-altaischen Sprachverwandtschaft* (Wiesbaden, 1962).
Gabinskij, M. A., *Vozniknovenie infinitiva kak vtoričnyj balkanskij jazykovoj process. Na materiale albanskogo jazyka* (Leningrad, 1967).
Gabka, K., "Zur Abgrenzung lexikalischer, morphologischer und syntaktischer Synonymie", *ZfSl* XII (1967), 727-734.
Garvin, P. L., [Review of] L. Hjelmslev, *Prolegomena to a Theory of Language*, *Lg* XXX (1954), 69-96.

Georgiev, V., "Le problème de l'union linguistique balkanique", in: *Actes du Premier Congrès international des études balkaniques et sud-est européennes*, VI (Sofia, 1968), 7-19.

Greenberg, J., "Some Methods of Dynamic Comparison in Linguistics", in: *Substance and Structure of Language*, 147-203.

Greenberg, J. H., "The Nature and Uses of Linguistic Typologies", *International Journal of American Linguistics* XXIII (1957), 68-77.

Hall, R. A., Jr., *An Essay on Language* (Philadelphia, 1968).

Halle, M., "On the Role of Simplicity in Linguistic Descriptions", in: *Structure of Language and its Mathematical Aspects. Proceedings of the Twelfth Symposium in Applied Mathematics*, R. Jakobson, ed. (Providence, R. I., 1961), 89-94.

——, "Phonology in Generative Grammar", *Word* XVIII (1962), 54-72 (reprinted in: *The Structure of Language*, 334-352).

[Xalle, M. =] Halle, M., "O pravilax russkogo sprjaženija", in: *American Contributions to the Fifth International Congress of Slavists*, I, 113-132.

Hamm, J., "Die Verschiebung der Velarkonsonanten", *Wiener slavistisches Jahrbuch* XV (1969), 38-58.

Harris, Z., "Co-occurrence and Transformation in Linguistic Structure", *Lg* XXXIII (1957), 283-340 (reprinted in: *The Structure of Language*, 155-210).

——, "Distributional Structure", *Word* X (1954), 146-162 (reprinted in: *The Structure of Language*, 33-49).

——, "Discourse Analysis", *Lg* XXVIII (1952), 1-30 (reprinted in: *The Structure of Language*, 355-383).

Haugen, E., "Directions in Modern Linguistics", *Lg* XXVII (1951), 211-222.

——, *Language Conflict and Language Planning: The Case of Modern Norwegian* (Cambridge, Mass., 1966).

——, "Linguistics and Language Planning" (with discussion), in: *Sociolinguistics. Proceedings of the UCLA Sociolinguistics Conference, 1964*, W. Bright, ed. (The Hague-Paris), 1966, 50-71.

——, "Semicommunication: The Language Gap in Scandinavia", *Sociological Inquiry* XXXVI (1966), 280-297.

Hjelmslev, L., "Dans quelle mesure les significations des mots peuvent-elles être considérées comme formant une structure?", in: *Proceedings of the Eighth International Congress of Linguists*, 636-654 (reprinted under the title "Pour une sémantique structurale" in: L. Hjelmslev, *Essais linguistiques*, 96-112).

——, *Essais linguistiques* (Copenhagen, 1959).

——, "Langue et parole", *Cahiers F. de Saussure* II (1943), 29-44 (reprinted in: *Essais linguistiques*, 69-81).

——, "La stratification du langage", *Word* X (1954), 163-188 (reprinted in: *Essais linguistiques*, 36-68).

——, "Pour une sémantique structurale", see "Dans quelle mesure ..."

——, *Prolegomena to a Theory of Language*, rev. English ed. (Madison, 1961).

——, *Sproget: En introduktion*, Copenhagen, 1963; French translation: *Le langage: Une introduction*, translated by M. Olsen, with a preface by A. J. Greimas (Paris, 1966).

Hockett, C. F., *A Course in Modern Linguistics* (New York, 1958).

——, *The State of the Art* (The Hague, 1968).

——, "Two Models of Grammatical Description", *Word* X (1954), 210-234.

Hoenigswald, H. M., *Language Change and Linguistic Reconstruction* (Chicago, 1959).

Holk, A. G. F., van, *The Semantic Spectrum of the Russian Infinitive* (Leiden, 1953).

IJSLP = *International Journal of Slavic Linguistics and Poetics.*

In honorem Endzelini (Chicago, 1960).

Ivanov, V. V., [Discussion of] R. Jakobson, "Typological Studies and Their Contribution to Historical Comparative Linguistics", in: *Proceedings of the Eighth International Congress of Linguists*, 25-27.

——, *Obščeindoevropejskaja, praslavjanskaja i anatolijskaja jazykovye sistemy (sravnital'no-tipologičeskie očerki)* (Moscow, 1965).

——, and V. N. Toporov, "K postanovke voprosa o drevnejšix otnošenijax baltijskix i slavjanskix jazykov", in: *Issledovanija po slavjanskomu jazykoznaniju* (Moscow, 1961), 273-305.

——, "K rekonstrukcii praslavjanskogo teksta", in: *Slavjanskoe jazykoznanie. Doklady sovetskoj delegacii. V Meždunarodnyj s"ezd slavistov*, 88-158.

——, *Slavjanskie modelirujuščie semiotičeskie sistemy (Drevnij period)*, Moscow, 1965.

Jakobson, R. O., "Morfologičeskie nabljudenija nad slavjanskim skloneniem (Sostav russkix padežnyx form)", with an English summary, in: *American Contributions to the Fourth International Congress of Slavicists* (The Hague, 1958), 127-156.

Jakobson, R., "Quest for the Essence of Language", *Diogenes* LI (Fall 1965), 21-37.

——, "Russian Conjugation", *Word* IV (1948), 155-167.

——, *Selected Writings*, I: *Phonological Studies* (The Hague, 1962).

——, *Sound and Meaning* (forthcoming).

——, "Typological Studies and Their Contribution to Historical Comparative Linguistics", in: *Proceedings of the Eighth International Congress of Linguists*, 17-35 (including discussion; reprinted in: R. Jakobson, *Selected Writings*, I, 523-530, without discussion).

Jeżowa, M., *Z problemów tak zwanej trzeciej palatalizacji tylnojęzykowych w językach słowiańskich* (Wrocław-Warsaw-Cracow, 1968).

Katz, J. J., "Recent Issues in Semantic Theory", *Foundations of Language* III (1967), 124-194.

——, and J. A. Fodor, "The Structure of a Semantic Theory", *Lg* XXXIX (1963), 170-210 (reprinted in: *The Structure of Language*, 479-518).

Kazazis, K., "On a Generative Grammar of the Balkan Languages", *Foundations of Language* III (1967), 117-123.

——, *Some Balkan Constructions Corresponding to Western European Infinitives*, Indiana University, 1965 (unpublished doctoral dissertation).

Kiparsky, V., *Russische historische Grammatik*, I (Heidelberg, 1963).

Klagstad, H. L., "Toward a Morpho-Syntactic Treatment of the Balkan Linguistic Group", in: *American Contributions to the Fifth International Congress of Slavists*, I, 179-189.

Klein, S., "Historical Change in Language Using Monte Carlo Techniques", *Mechanical Translation* IX (1966), 67-82.

Klima, E. S., "Relatedness between Grammatical Systems", *Lg* XL (1964), 1-20.

Knutsson, K., *Über die sogenannte zweite Palatalisierung in den slavischen Sprachen* (Lund, 1926).

Koschmieder, E., "Die noetischen Grundlagen der Syntax" = *Sitzungsberichte der Bayerischen Akademie der Wissenschaften, Philologisch-historische Klasse*, 4 (Munich, 1951) (reprinted in: E. Koschmieder, *Beiträge zur allgemeinen Syntax*, Heidelberg, 1965, 70-89).

Krahe, H., *Indogermanische Sprachwissenschaft*, II, 3rd ed. (Berlin, 1959).

Krause, W., *Handbuch des Gotischen*, 3rd ed. (Munich, 1968).

Kuryłowicz, J., "A propos de hittite *ḫ*: Réponse à une critique de M. W. Petersen", *BSL* XXXVI (1935), 25-27.

——, *Études indoeuropéennes*, I (Cracow, 1935).

——, "*ə* indoeuropéen et *ḫ* hittite", in: *Symbolae grammaticae in honorem J. Rozwadowski*, I (Cracow, 1927), 95-104.

——, "On the Methods of Internal Reconstruction" (with discussion), in: *Proceedings of the Ninth International Congress of Linguists*, 9-36.

Lakoff, G., "Instrumental Adverbs and the Concept of Deep Structure", *Foundations of Language* IV (1968), 4-29.

Lakoff, G. P. and J. R. Ross, "Is Deep Structure Necessary?" (Cambridge, Mass., 1967) (mimeographed).

Lakoff, R. T., *Abstract Syntax and Latin Complementation* (Cambridge, Mass., 1968).

Lamb, S. M., "Epilegomena to a Theory of Language", *Romance Philology* XIX (1966), 531-573.

——, "Lexicology and Semantics", in: *Linguistics Today*, 40-49.

——, *Outline of Stratificational Grammar* (Washington, D.C., 1966).

Lehmann, W. P., *Historical Linguistics: an Introduction* (New York, 1962).

[Leman, U. F. =] Lehmann, W. P., "Vyvody o protoindoevropejskoj glagol'-noj sisteme, osnovannye na vnutrennem analize sanskrita", *VJa* 1961: 2, 24-27.

Lekomceva, M. I., D. M. Segal, T. M. Sudnik, S. M. Šur, "Opyt postroenija fonologičeskoj tipologii blizkorodstvennyx jazykov", in: *Slavjanskoe jazykoznanie. Doklady sovetskoj delegacii. V Meždunarodnyj s"ezd slavistov* (Moscow, 1963), 423-476.

Levenston, E. and J. O. Ellis, "A Transfer-Grammar Development of System-Reduction Quantified Method", *Zeitschrift für Phonetik, Sprachwissenschaft und Kommunikationsforschung* XVI (1964), 449-452.

Lewy, E., "Der Bau der europäischen Sprachen", in: *Proceedings of the Royal Irish Academy* XLVIII, C (1942/3), 15-117.

Lg = *Language*.

[Lajtner, T. M. =] Lightner, T. M., "O cikličeskix pravilax v russkom sprjaženii", *VJa* 1965: 2, 45-54.

——, "Ob alternacii *e ∾ o* v sovremennom russkom literaturnom jazyke", *VJa* 1966: 5, 64-80.

Lightner, T. M., "On the Phonology of the Old Church Slavonic Conjugation", *IJSLP* X (1966), 1-28.

——, "Preliminary Remarks on the Morphophonemic Component of Polish", in: *Quarterly Progress Report, MIT Research Laboratory of Electronics* LXXI (1963), 220-235.

Linguistics Today = *Linguistics Today*, A. A. Hill, ed. (New York-London, 1969).

Lomtev, T. P., *Očerki po istoričeskomu sintaksisu russkogo jazyka* (Moscow, 1956).

Malmberg, B., *Structural Linguistics and Human Communication* (New York-Berlin, 1963).

——, "Synchronie et diachronie", in: *Actes du Xe Congrès international des linguistes*, I (Bucharest, 1969), 13-36 (including discussion).

Mareš, F. V., *The Origin of the Slavic Phonological System and Its Development up to the End of Slavic Language Unity* (Ann Arbor, 1965).

Martinet, A., "Réflexions sur les universaux du langage", *FL* I (1967), 125-134.

McCawley, J. D., "Concerning the Base Component of a Transformational Grammar", *Foundations of Language* IV (1968), 243-269.

——, "The Role of Semantics in a Grammar", in: *Universals in Linguistic Theory*, 124-169.

Milewski, T., *Językoznawstwo* (Warsaw, 1965).

Mrázek, R., "Dedukce a empirie při srovnávací typologii slovanské věty", in: *Otázky slovanské syntaxe*, II: *Sborník symposia "Strukturní typy slovanské věty a jejich vyvoj", Brno 20.-22. X. 1966* (Brno, 1968), 185-200.

Orzechowska, H., "Zjawiska wtórnej archaizacji w bułgarskim języku literackim (Z historii zanikania podwójnych dopełnień)", in: *Z polskich studiów slawistycznych*, 3: *Językoznawstwo* (Warsaw, 1968), 139-151.

Peškovskij, A. M., *Russkij sintaksis v naučnom osveščenii*, 7th ed. (Moscow, 1956).

Petrovici, E., *Kann das Phonemsystem einer Sprache durch fremden Einfluss umgestaltet werden? Zum slavischen Einfluss auf das rumänische Lautsystem* (The Hague, 1957).

Postal, P. M., *Aspects of Phonological Theory* (New York, 1968).

——, "Underlying and Superficial Linguistic Structure", *Harvard Educational Review* XXXIV (1964), 246-266 (reprinted in: *Language and Learning*, J. A. Emig, J. T. Fleming, H. M. Popp, eds., New York, 1966, 153-175).

Proceedings of the Eighth International Congress of Linguists (also with French title) (Oslo, 1958).

Proceedings of the Ninth International Congress of Linguists, H. G. Lunt, ed. (The Hague, 1964).

Puhvel, J., ed., see *Substance and Structure of Language*.

Pulgram, E., "Trends and Predictions", in *To Honor Roman Jakobson*, II (The Hague, 1967), 1634-1649.

Rakstu krājums veltījums Jānim Endzelīnam vina 85 dzives un 65 darba gadu atcerei (Riga, 1959).

Reichenkron, G., "Der Typus der Balkansprachen", *ZfBalk* I (1962), 91-122.

Revzin, I. I., *Metod modelirovanija i tipologija slavjanskix jazykov* (Moscow, 1967).

Roždestvenskij, Ju. V. [Review of] B. A. Uspenskij, *Strukturnaja tipologija jazykov*, *VJa* 1966: 3, 111-115.

Růžička, R., *Studien zur Theorie der russischen Syntax* (Berlin, 1966).

——, "Zur syntaktischen Typologie moderner slawischer Literatursprachen", *ZfSl* VIII (1963), 833-860.

Sadnik, L. and R. Aitzetmüller, *Handwörterbuch zu den altkirchenslavischen Texten* (Heidelberg-The Hague, 1955).
Sandfeld, K., *Linguistique balkanique. Problèmes et résultats* (Paris, 1930).
Saporta, S., "Ordered Rules, Dialect Differences, and Historical Processes", *Lg* XLI (1965), 218-224.
Schröpfer, J., "Zur inneren Sprachform der Balkanvölker", *ZfSl* I (1956), 139-151.
ScSl = *Scando-Slavica*.
Seidel, E., "Zur Problematik des Sprachbundes", in: *Beiträge zur Sprachwissenschaft ... W. Steinitz zum 60. Geburtstag*, 372-381.
Senn, A., *Handbuch der litauischen Sprache*, I: *Grammatik* (Heidelberg, 1966).
——, "The Relationship of Baltic and Slavic", in *Ancient Indo-European Dialects*, 139-151.
Shevelov, G. Y., *A Prehistory of Slavic: The Historical Phonology of Common Slavic* (Heidelberg, 1964) (and New York, 1965).
Sigurd, B., "Generative Grammar and Historical Linguistics", *Acta Linguistica Hafniensia* X (1966), 35-48.
Slavjanskoe jazykoznanie. Doklady sovetskoj delegacii. V Meždunarodnyj s"ezd slavistov (*Sofija, sentjabr' 1963*) (Moscow, 1963).
Sravnitel'no-istoričeskij sintaksis vostočnoslavjanskix jazykov: Členy predloženija, V. I. Borkovskij, ed. (Moscow, 1968).
Substance and Structure of Language, J. Puhvel, ed. (Berkeley-Los Angeles, 1969).
Suxotin, V. P., *Sintaksičeskaja sinonimika v sovremennom russkom literaturnom jazyke: Glagol'nye slovosočetanija* (Moscow, 1960).
Šaumjan, S. K., "Concerning the Logical Basis of Linguistic Theory", in: *Proceedings of the Ninth International Congress of Linguists*, 155-160.
——, *Strukturnaja lingvistika* (Moscow, 1965).
The Structure of Language. Readings in the Philosophy of Language, J. A. Fodor, J. J. Katz, eds. (Englewood Cliffs, N.J., 1964).
Toporov, V. N., "Nekotorye soobraženija otnositel'no izučenija istorii praslavjanskogo jazyka", in: *Slavjanskoe jazykoznanie. Sbornik statej* (Moscow, 1959), 3-27.
Trautmann, R., *Baltisch-Slavisches Wörterbuch* (Göttingen, 1923).
Universals in Linguistic Theory, E. Bach, R. T. Harms, eds. (New York, 1968).
Uspenskij, B. A., "Lingvističeskaja žizn' Kopengagena", *VJa* 1962: 3, 148-151.
——, *Nekotorye voprosy strukturnoj tipologii. Avtoreferat kandidatskoj dissertacii* (Moscow, 1963).
——, *Principy strukturnoj tipologii*, Moscow, 1962; English translation: *Principles of Structural Typology* (The Hague-Paris, 1968).
——, *Strukturnaja tipologija jazykov* (Moscow, 1965).
——, "Tipologičeskaja klassifikacija jazykov kak osnova jazykovyx sootvetstvij (Struktura jazyka-ètalona pri tipologičeskoj klassifikacii jazykov)", *VJa* 1961: 6, 51-64.
Vaillant, A., *Grammaire comparée des langues slaves*, I (Lyon-Paris, 1950).
——, [Review of] G. Y. Shevelov, *A Prehistory of Slavic: The Historical Phonology of Common Slavic*, *BSL* LX (1965), 52-81.
Van Campen, J., "On the Appearance of a New Work on Common Slavic Phonology (A Review Article)", *IJSLP* X (1966), 52-81.

VJa = *Voprosy jazykoznanija.*

Volockaja, Z. M., T. N. Mološnaja, I. I. Revzin, T. V. Civ'jan, "Ob odnom podxode k tipologii slavjanskix jazykov (na materiale sistemy sklonenija suščestvitel'nogo)", in: *Slavjanskoe jazykoznanie. Doklady sovetskoj delegacii. V Meždunarodnyj s"ezd slavistov*, 510-552.

Watkins, C., "Italo-Celtic Revisited", in: *Ancient Indo-European Dialects*, 29-50.

——, "Preliminaries to the Reconstruction of Indo-European Sentence Structure" (with discussion), in: *Proceedings of the Ninth International Congress of Linguists*, 1035-1045.

Weiher, E., "Urslavisch-Gemeinslavisch-Dialekte des Gemeinslavischen (?)", *Anzeiger für slavische Philologie* II (1967), 82-100.

Weinreich, U., "Explorations in Semantic Theory", in: *Current Trends*, III, 395-477.

——, "On the Compatibility of Genetic Relationship and Convergent Development", *Word* XIV (1958), 374-379.

——, "Problems in the Analysis of Idioms", in: *Substance and Structure of Language*, 23-81.

Wessén, E., *Om det tyska inflytandet på svenskt språk under medeltiden* (Stockholm, 1954).

Whitfield, F., "Glossematics", in: *Linguistics Today*, 250-258.

——, "Louis Hjelmslev" (Obituary), *Lg* XLII (1966), 615-619.

Wittgenstein, L., *Philosophical Investigations* (Oxford, 1953).

Worth, D. S., "On the Morphophonemics of the Slavic Verb", *Slavia*, XXXIX (1970), 1-9.

——, "'Surface Structure' and 'Deep Structure' in Slavic Morphology", in: *American Contributions to the Sixth International Congress of Slavists*, I, 395-427.

——, "Transform Analysis of Russian Instrumental Constructions", *Word* XIV (1958), 247-290; Russian translation: "Transformacionnyj analiz konstrukcij s tvoritel'nym padežom v russkom jazyke", in: *Novoe v lingvistike*, II, V. A. Zvegincev, ed. (Moscow, 1962), 637-683.

Zaliznjak, A. A., "O vozmožnoj svjazi meždu operacionnymi ponjatijami sinxronnogo opisanija i diaxroniej", in: *Simpozium po strukturnomu izučeniju znakovyx sistem* (Moscow, 1962) (not available for page reference).

——, "Sinxronnoe opisanie i vnutrennjaja rekonstrukcija", in: *Problemy sravnitel'noj grammatiki indoevropejskix jazykov. Naučnaja sessija. Tezisy dokladov* (Moscow, 1964), 51-54.

Zeps, V. J., "A Synchronic and Diachronic Order of Rules: Mutations of Velars in Old Church Slavonic", in: *Approaches in Linguistic Methodology*, I. Rauch and C. T. Scott, eds. (Madison-Milwaukee-London, 1967), 145-151.

ZfBalk = *Zeitschrift für Balkanologie.*
ZfSl = *Zeitschrift für Slawistik.*
ZfslPh = *Zeitschrift für slavische Philologie.*

The monograph *Operators and Nucleus. A Contribution to the Theory of Grammar* by P. A. M. Seuren (= *Cambridge Studies in Linguistics*, 2) and the contribution "Grammatische Kategorie und typologische Forschungen" by M. M. Guchman (in: *Zeichen und System der Sprache*, III, G. F. Meier, ed., Berlin, 1966, 262-273), both bearing upon the subject matter discussed in my paper "Deep Structure and Typological Linguistics", and the paper by D. Cohen, "Why the Slavic 'Second Palatalization' Comes First" (in: *Papers from the Fifth Regional Meeting*, Chicago Linguistic Society, April 18-19, 1969, Department of Linguistics, University of Chicago, R. I. Binnick, A. Davison, G. M. Green, J. L. Morgan, eds., 306-313), relevant to my study "Internal Reconstruction, Order of Synchronic Rules in Generative Grammar, and the Problem of Early Balto-Slavic Relations", were not yet available to me when the manuscript of this volume was submitted for publication.